Steps in Understanding

A course in active comprehension

BOOK 1

Mike Hamlin

Hutchinson

London Melbourne Sydney Auckland Johannesburg

Contents

Introduction

As experienced teachers are aware, many children soon learn to treat comprehension exercises as irrelevant chores which they have to complete to satisfy someone else. A major shift is needed towards methods which encourage pupils to interrogate and interact with texts for a variety of their *own* purposes, to make sense of what they are reading by questioning it against what they already know.

It is also important that the texts themselves should be worthwhile — stories, poems and other materials which speak directly and powerfully to the age group. The material selected needs to be recognizable and direct, but also to some extent puzzling and open to alternative interpretation.

All this is not to argue that guidelines and structures are unnecessary; far from it. Clearly presented, yet flexible, frameworks are often essential if pupils are to enter texts with any degree of self-confidence. *Steps in Understanding* should therefore be seen as practically developing some of the recommendations first raised by the 'Effective Use of Reading' Project and especially their 'Directed Activities Related to Texts' (DARTS).

The central aim of this series of books is to motivate pupils to reflect critically on stories, poems and non-literary texts. To this end, the course brings together material that is lively, engaging and worth spending time on. A range of actively questioning approaches encourages pupils to explore texts for themselves and to find their own routes to more satisfying answers.

Moreover, the techniques suggested are eminently suitable as preparation for 'course-work' submissions in comprehension, as in, for example, the GCSE examination at 16+.

The Author
Mike Hamlin is an experienced teacher of English in colleges and schools. Currently Head of Media Education at Toot Hill Comprehensive, Nottingham, he is also Assistant Chief Examiner in English Comprehension at 16+ for the Northern Examining Association. He is the author (with David Jackson) of *Making Sense Of Comprehension* (Macmillan, 1984).

1 | *First impressions*

When we read a new story, all the characters are being shown to us for the first time. Our first reactions when reading are often the most important: they provide a sort of framework around which the story can grow.

Read this opening chapter, 'The Best of Enemies', from a book by Robert Leeson called *Challenge in the Dark*.

I

The Best of Enemies

Monday morning. Dad came yawning up the stairs as I came yawning down. He was coming off night shift ready for a good day's sleep. I was starting my first week at the big school. I'd have gladly changed places, but they don't take you on British Rail at eleven.

We dodged about on the stairs trying to get past each other. Then he said:

"Do your best, Mike."

"OK, Dad."

I did my best, too. Before my first week at the new school was over I had two nightmares, a black eye and was nearly trapped ten feet underground. But I'm telling this too fast. Back to Monday.

Mum was in the kitchen. Our Sis had rushed off to work early for some strange reason. So I didn't get any sarky remarks from her. That helped.

"Have you got your dinner money?"

"Yes, Mum," I splurted.

"Don't talk with your mouth full, love."

"Yes, Mum."

"Have you got your plimsolls?"

"Yes – No, Mum, have I heckaslike. We don't need them today."

"Don't swear."

"Heckaslike isn't swearing."

"I don't like it anyway."

"All right, Mum."

"Have you got your key? I may be out when you get home."

"Yes, Mum."

Mum came along our road and down Station Road with me. Then she turned off along High Street to the offices where she goes cleaning. She wasn't thrilled about that but she had to do it. That's how I felt about the new school.

Mum gave me a kiss. I sneaked a look round. There were some kids on the other side of Station Road, but they didn't see anything. I don't think.

"Look after yourself, Mike."

I whipped across the road by the station and walked along by the shops. I wanted to get a fun-sized chocolate bar from the newsagents, to keep my strength up till break time. Fun-sized. They mean small. Why can't they say so?

The shop was packed, but I couldn't see anyone I knew from our old school. That was the trouble. My mate Ranji wasn't coming up till next year. He's six months younger than me, though you can't tell. My other friend, Sandra, is thirteen and she doesn't go to the comprehensive. Her Dad sends her to St Winifred's. He thinks it's a good influence on her and we're not. Fat lot he knows. Anyway, he's away from home half the time and she's got no Mum, so she has to look after her brother Andrew. He's a pain, Andy, only eight, but big as a baby elephant. And everywhere we go, he goes. Like it or lump it, says Sandra. So we lump it.

But I wouldn't see any of them till the weekend. Baxter man, you're on your own for the week. And didn't I know it.

Before I realized, I was in School Lane, pushing about among a big crowd of kids, all my own age. The older ones were coming in later, so we had the big school to ourselves for the morning. They call it the big school – well, because it's bigger. Everything's bigger – the yard, the buildings, the stairs, even the teachers. And as soon as we all got into the yard, this voice came over the loudspeaker system.

"Wha-ha-haw-haw-hoo-hoo-ha," it went.

"Eh, what was that?" I asked a lad standing next to me.

"Do not resist or you will be annihilated," he answered.

Very funny.

I could see this place was going to be dodgey. Instead of staying in one classroom all the time, you trail round with your gear from one place to another.

And in each room you get a different teacher. Where do they get them all from? How can you tell them apart? I began to panic. But then we were all called into the assembly hall and sat down. I could see one or two people I recognized now, but they were farther away in different groups. I was in 1J.

A teacher at the front started talking to us. I found out afterwards he was The Voice – the one who made those weird noises over the tannoy. But he sounded almost normal right now.

He rambled on about the school, how it used to be a grammar until they changed it, so that anyone could come there.

"Oh ah, even nits like Baxter."

What was that? I could hear somebody having a giggle behind me and sneaked a look round. I didn't fancy what I saw. About a row back was someone from our old school, with one of his mates. He was Steven Taylor. I knew him all right – and I wished I didn't. Steven Taylor's thin and pale, and his face is like a ferret's with a sharp nose and red eyes.

I'd run across him more than once – trying to get at me, needling me for one reason or another. I could take it in the old school because I had my mates. But here I was on my own. And just my luck to have him and his mates in my class. This *was* going to be dodgey – I could feel it.

Still this school was a big place. I'd just have to keep out of his way. I pretended I'd heard nothing.

The rest of the day went quickly and I began to get the hang of the school, where the assembly hall was, where the dining-hall was, where the labs were, where the lavs were – even they were bigger.

They let us out at three o'clock that first day and I got into School Lane smartish. I passed cocky Steven Taylor nattering to his friends, showing off. In fact he was so fond of the sound of his own voice he didn't even notice me. I shot off up School Lane and into Station Road. Steven Taylor lived near the railway and I lived farther up the hill, near the Park. So, once I was over the railway bridge I was on home ground, more or less.

That day I was in luck, because Mum was home after all. She'd got off work early and was busy at the cooker.

"How did it go, lad?"

I flopped down at the table.

"Is that fish fingers, Mum?"

"Get your coat off, wash your hands and I'll tell you."

"Ah, it's fish fingers, I can smell it."

"The lad's a genius. That's modern education for you."

My sister, Laura, came barging in through the kitchen door. I blew her a raspberry.

"Education's wasted on some people," I said.

"Give over, you two," said Mum. "Somebody put the kettle on."

Our Sis disappeared. She's crafty. I filled the kettle at the sink and Dad came into the room, half asleep and rubbing his eyes.

"Now, Mike, how did it go?"

"Oh, all right, Dad. Hey, it isn't half big that place."

"Ah, think you'll like it, Mike?"

"I think so."

Mum put the fish fingers in front of me. I remembered I was hungry – only a chocolate bar and a fun-sized school dinner since dawn. The fish fingers were hot and burned my tongue as I swallowed.

"Aaargh," I said.

"Manners you pig," said our Sis, coming back into the kitchen. She put on a posh voice. "Is that what they teach you at Bugletown Comprehensive?"

"Oh, get—."

"That's enough, Mik ," said Mum.

"Ah, let's have a bit of peace," said Dad, pouring out the tea.

When we'd finished eating, Dad put the telly on. I sat there watching and feeling comfortable. Then I remembered Steven Taylor.

Well, I thought. I'll just keep out of his way. It's a big place, after all.

But I was wrong. It wasn't quite big enough.

Now answer the following questions:

1 List the five main characters shown to us in the chapter.

2 Design a 'Personal Profile' card for each character. Start with the headings 'Name', 'Age', 'Occupation'. Then add 'Likes' and 'Dislikes', as well as any other headings you can think of. Under each heading, write in the information you have learned about that character. Add a brief description or portrait of the character, as well as any other interesting thoughts and comments. Your profile cards could look something like this:

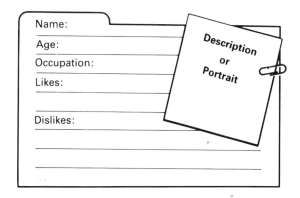

Remember to base your profiles on the information, suggestions and clues contained in 'The Best of Enemies'. But you may have to build on these starting points yourself – just remember that your additional ideas should fit the character you are profiling.

Look closely at the conversation between Mike and his mother early on in the story (page 5) and the conversation between the whole Baxter family towards the end of the chapter (pages 8–9).

Think back to some similar moments with *your* family, say at a busy breakfast or tea time.

- 1 Give three examples of the sort of things that happen.

- 2 Give three examples of the sort of things that are said.

- 3 Make a list of at least four family phrases that regularly crop up at times like these. For example:
  'Aren't you ready yet?'
  'If I've told you once, I've told you a thousand times.'
  'You are not going out dressed like that, young lady.'

- 4 Using your list as a starting point, write out some typical family conversations of your own. Try to make them sound as realistic as you can.

In the picture story which follows, several words have been blanked out.

Read through the picture story.

Now answer the following questions:

1 Using the clues provided by the pictures and the remaining words to help you, write down the word which you think best fills each gap.
(a) Start by making a list of a few possible words for each gap.
(b) Then choose the word which you think fits best.

2 When you have finished, you can compare your choice of words with that of others in your group. You can also compare them with the original words, which can be found on page 106.

Follow on. . .

● 1 We learn from the picture story that the class from Platt's Road Middle School are going to visit Shawfield Square the following Wednesday. Continue the story, either as a story or as a play script. If the last three frames of the picture story were written as a play script, it would look something like this:

Teacher: (cheerfully) Right, next Wednesday, this class is going down to Shawfield Square to _____ things.
Andy: (smiling) On walls, Sir? (thinking of walls covered with graffiti)
Teacher: (angrily) No, Andy, not on walls. In books.

Andy: (still smiling) We won't need our _____ _____, then? (rest of children giggle and smirk in background)

Now, over to you.

● 2 (a) Sketch or quickly copy out the fifteen picture frames, but this time leave out all of the speech.
(b) Change the order of the frames and add new speech to create an original story of your own. Try to create at least two different stories in this way.

$\boxed{3}$ Making sense of 'Wildtrack'

Read through the magazine article on the next page a couple of times, quickly but carefully. (Ignore the 'Fact and Fiction' column for the moment.)

When you have read the article twice, cover it with a sheet of paper. **Now answer the following questions** to see how much information has stayed with you. You can answer the questions by yourself, or you may prefer to work in small groups.

1 (a) What is the most likely form of death for any town fox?
   (b) When is it illegal to offer fox cubs for sale?
   (c) What tends to happen when 'pet' foxes grow older?
   (d) What is Wildtrack's advice to anyone finding an abandoned fox cub?

2 Take the paper away and see which answers you got right.
   (a) Was it difficult to remember what you had read?
   (b) Which sections were the most difficult to remember?
   (c) Which sections were the easiest to remember?
   (d) What do you think are the reasons for some sections being easy to remember and other sections being difficult?

3 The magazine article was attempting to be entertaining and informative at the same time.
   (a) How entertaining was the article?
   (b) How informative was it?
   (c) Do you think it managed to combine the two elements successfully? Explain your answer.
   (d) Suggest ways in which you think the article might have been presented in a better way.

4 Using some of the information in the article to help you, design a simple, attractive leaflet which warns people your age against 'adopting' fox cubs.

Follow on . . .

● 1 Look at the 'Fact and Fiction' part of the page.
   (a) Write down the seven true or false statements on a piece of paper. As a survey, ask as many people as you can whether they believe each statement to be true or false. Keep a note of their answers.
   (b) Using the information you have collected in your survey, draw a chart to show the things people know and don't know about foxes in towns.

Wild track

'ADOPTING' FOX CUBS
The sad truth

The second part of producer Mike Beynon's look at foxes.

TOWN FOXES:
FACT AND FICTION

Town foxes are half-starved.
FALSE
The average urban fox is better fed than its rural cousin.

Town foxes are disease-ridden.
FALSE
Although mange is occasionally found, most town foxes are healthy. Foxes, by the way, don't carry their own fleas.

At this time of year people occasionally come across lone fox cubs. Maybe the vixen has been killed by a motor car – the most likely form of death for any town fox – or dogs have killed or split up the fox family.

On one occasion, in a pub in Bristol, a man came in carrying a fox cub – no more than 10 days old – which some teenagers had dug out of its earth. He was trying to sell it, but soon got a rocket from me.

There were even adverts in newspapers last year offering fox cubs for sale! Unfortunately that's not illegal, unless there's any cruelty involved, in which case such people could be prosecuted.

But beware! It's all deceptive. You're planting the seeds of that fox's death, because you're taking away its fear of humans and dogs. Just imagine if that fox is released back into the wild, and one day sees a dog, rushes up to it and starts to play. It'll probably be killed. In fights between dogs and foxes, it's always the fox that comes off worst.

BORN FREE – STAY FREE

Also, a wild fox has to *learn* to kill for food. It's not purely instinct. A captive fox will not know how to hunt and may die of starvation.

For the family, too, life is going to be difficult as the fox grows up. It will stop being a friendly plaything and start to become an unpredictable and possibly dangerous animal, especially when there's any food about. Children could be at risk.

The family will want to get rid of the young fox.

The choices are to find an animal sanctuary that will take it, have the animal put down, or keep it in captivity for the rest of its life!

So perhaps it's not surprising that *Wildtrack*'s advice, to anyone finding an abandoned fox cub is to leave it where it is. Apart from anything else, vixens often leave cubs to stray while they are out hunting. But she will return for it and take it back to their earth or burrow.

Foxes come into town from the countryside at night.
FALSE
Town foxes actually *live* in the town.

Foxes kill chickens.
TRUE
Foxes will certainly kill chickens and other fowl. But they also get blamed for deaths caused by other animals; cats and dogs, for instance, as well as stoats and weasels.

Foxes kill cats.
FALSE
Very little evidence of this.

Foxes will attack people.
FALSE
Simply untrue.

Foxes are cunning, sly and devious.
That's what the storybooks say, but what they mean is that the fox is clever, learns quickly and adapts well. That's why urban foxes are thriving.

Later this summer, you'll see the inevitable stories in newspapers about how somebody is bringing up a fox cub. The accompanying picture will probably show the cub with a cat, puppy, duck, adoring child or whatever. 'How extraordinary! How unusual!' scream the captions.

IN CAPTIVITY

It's the easiest thing in the world to take a fox cub home, but the catch is you'll probably be condemning that animal to death!

If the fox cub is very tiny, still with its eyes closed, it has to be fed frequently with the right kind of milk. It needs certain vitamins and minerals to help it to grow properly.

In the wild, the vixen would lick the cub's bottom to stimulate it to defecate. That's important, otherwise the cub could quickly become constipated and die. So in captivity, it's equally important to wipe its bottom with cotton wool and warm water. Not everybody's cup of tea!

Once the cub is weaned on to solid food it becomes easier. They're very like young dogs at first, playing all the time, making friends with the family pets, being stroked and cuddled by everybody.

17

Your chart might look something like this:

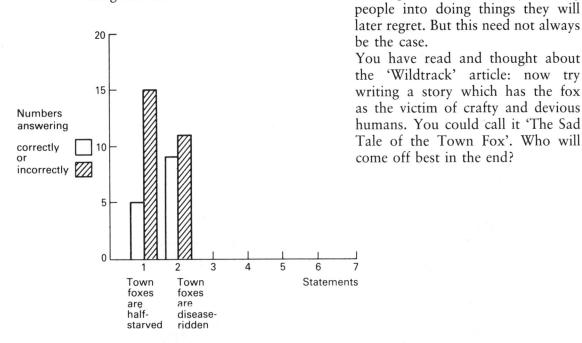

(c) Write down what you have learned through doing this survey.

● 2 Story-books often show foxes as sly, cunning creatures, cleverly tricking people into doing things they will later regret. But this need not always be the case.

You have read and thought about the 'Wildtrack' article: now try writing a story which has the fox as the victim of crafty and devious humans. You could call it 'The Sad Tale of the Town Fox'. Who will come off best in the end?

4 | *What comes next?* *(Epidode 1)*

This short story by Nicholas Fisk has been broken into seven episodes. After each episode, quickly write down your impressions of what you have just read. Use the following headings:

Things you liked

Things you disliked

Things that interested you

Things that surprised you

Things that confused you

Then, just before going on to read the next instalment, briefly write down what you think will happen next.

You will find that there are several things happening at the same time in this story. Don't worry, they will all come together in the end, if you keep your wits about you!

If you repeat your impressions for each of the seven episodes and also add a final comment at the end, you will have built up an interesting 'Reading Log' for the story as a whole.

Here is Episode 1.

The Boy the Dog and the Spaceship

by Nicholas Fisk

A There was a boy and his dog, running and rolling and chasing in a field.

*   *   *

B There was a spaceship hurtling through nothingness, most of its crew already dead, and the rest despairingly fighting on to make landfall on a strange planet.

*   *   *

The boy's name was Kevin. He was twelve. His dog was called Reg. He was young too. Boy and dog understood each other perfectly.

C Kevin shouted 'Devil dog!' and pounced at Reg. Reg rolled his eyes, yelped with delight and pranced off sideways. Kevin chased Reg until he was tired out. Then they sat down together, side by side in the evening shadows. When they had got their breath back, Kevin shouted 'Devil dog!' and the chase started all over again.

19

In the spaceship, the Captain contacted the Engineer. The channel was live — the Captain could hear the slight echoing hiss from the speaker — yet the Engineer did not respond.

The Captain barked, 'Report. I want your report. Make your report.'

The Engineer's breathing changed. It turned into long sobs. 'Report.'

The Engineer spoke. 'It's no good, Captain, it's no good . . . ! The heat's burned out the bounce beam, the retros have gone dead. We'll just hit, Captain. We're going to smash.'

*   *   *

D Seconds later, the retros bellowed and the ship checked so violently that the Captain fell over. He got up bleeding. He said, 'Engineer!' then noticed the Engineer's light had died which meant that the Engineer had died. So he called the In-Flight Tech.

'In-flight, we have full retro, am I correct?'

'Eighty per cent retro, Captain. No more to come. But may be enough — '

'It must be enough.'

'Yes, Captain.'

'Very well. Crashball, In-Flight. And tell the others.'

'The others,' the Captain said to himself. 'Just two others. . . .'

He switched off and began to fit himself into the crashball cocoon. He fitted webbing harnesses over his body and buckled them. He pressed a button and padded arms enfolded him. A little tubular snake leapt from a padded hole and latched itself to a socket near his neck: his clothing began to swell, then the walls of the cocoon. The puffed surfaces met. Now he was completely encased in a puffy softness, pressing tighter and tighter.

He waited for the stab. It came. The needle darted itself into one of the Captain's veins. A drug entered his bloodstream. Almost immediately he felt drowsy and comfortable, but still alert. The same needle was connected to a whole junction of tiny tubes filled with his own blood and plasma; with stimulants, painkillers, curatives and other life givers and life adjusters; even with painless death.

'Check in,' said the Captain.

The In-Flight Tech and the Co-ordinator should have answered. Their lights were live. The Co-ordinator said, 'Excuse me, Captain, but I think I'm dying.' A moment later he died.

'In-Flight Tech,' said the Captain.

No answer.

'In-Flight Tech! Check in!'

'Yes, Captain?'

'Just checking,' said the Captain, and switched off so that the Tech should not hear his sigh of relief.

The ship hurtled on. It was still slowing, the Captain could feel it through the cocoons. In the control centre, the screens showed a green and blue planet with seas and clouds and land masses, coming nearer all the time. But there was no one outside the cocoons to watch the screens.

* * *

The boy whistled for his dog. 'Here boy!' he commanded, and whistled again. 'Come on, Reg.'

E Reg pranced and curvetted towards the boy, being silly. He wanted to make the boy laugh, but the boy was solemn. He was proud of having such a well trained dog. 'Good boy,' he said gravely, 'Good old Reg.'

A minute later, the boy and the dog were wrestling in the grass.

To start you thinking:

- 1 (a) How would you describe the play between the boy and his dog? Happy and familiar or solemn and unpredictable?
    (b) What *three* other words of your own would you choose to describe their play?

- 2 (a) Do you think the Captain will survive the crash?
    (b) Give reasons for your answer.

- 3 'A green and blue planet with seas and clouds and land masses' (section D). Which planet do you think this might be?

- 4 At this early stage, what do you think could be the links between the boy, the dog and the spaceship?

- 5 Now write down your first impressions of the whole episode. Remember the headings:

* Things you liked
* Things you disliked
* Things that interested you
* Things that surprised you
* Things that confused you
* What might happen next?
* Any other thoughts?

5 | *Making sense: 'The ant-lion'*

This is a complete short story by Judith Wright. First read the story through twice.

Now answer the following questions:

1 Make a list of all the words and phrases used by the writer to describe the ant-lion, especially its head and jaws.

2 One word is used in this way more than once. Which is it?

3 (a) Why do you think this word is repeated?
  (b) What does the word suggest to you?

4 Max and Morvenna are a boy and a girl. They behave and react very differently in the story. Draw two columns: one headed 'Max', the other headed 'Morvenna'. Then underneath, briefly list the main differences in their behaviour.

5 (a) Is this how boys and girls are *expected* to react to things?
  (b) Give reasons for your answer.

6 What do you think about the way they behave?

7 When Max drops the meat-ant into the little pit, the story continues:

'In their minds the ant and its arena of battle enlarged, filled the whole world. Under the sand at the pit-bottom crouched the lion, big as a real lion, waiting for the ant to slide down a little farther. But this one was so big; bigger than the ant-lion itself. Max said, "Now we'll see some sport." '

The children's imagination seems to have taken them somewhere else here. Where do you think they might be?

8 Look again at the end of the story – the twelve lines after 'Max sat up slowly.'. The children's mood seems to have changed. Why do you think they are behaving like this?

Follow on . . .

Sometimes, curiosity about animals or insects can get mixed up with a sort of cruelty; and before we realize it, we have done something we later regret.

Think back through your own memories, making rough notes if it helps. Then write up the story of one such incident, concentrating on how you *felt*, before, during and after the incident, rather than what you actually *did*.

The ant-lion

'He can't get it; he can't get a hold of it,' Morvenna cried.
She thrust suddenly with the end of a twig, trying to push
the ant up the shifting sand-slope of the pit. But her brother,
lying opposite her, filled his cheeks with air and blew hard.
The ant fell back to the pit-bottom, and in a moment the
little fury of jaws burst out at it, seized it, vanished again.
Only a flurry of sand in the bottom of the little pit marked
for a few seconds the ant's last struggle.

The two children sat up slowly, breathing again. They
looked at each other with a kind of guilt. Max's face was
quite red; Morvenna's mouth was open.

'How many would he kill, I wonder?' Max said. 'That's
three we've given him, but they were all little ones. I'll get
a meat-ant and see what he does.'

'Oh no, Max, don't, don't. I don't want you to.' Morvenna
clenched her hands, but she could not help looking round in
the grass for the meat-ant track that led to the ant-hill farther
up the slope. Max went across to it, holding his twig, and bent
down. Morvenna gave a scream. 'If you do, Maxie, I'll kill
the lion. I will, truly.'

'Don't you dare,' Max said. 'It's the first ant-lion we've
ever seen and we might never find another. I want to show it
to everyone.' He came back, holding his twig gingerly and
turning it from end to end as the red ant rushed along it.
Meat-ants could bite.

'Now I'll put it in,' he said. 'Look, Morv.' He shook the

twig hard over the little pit, but the ant was obstinate and clung. Angry, intent, he finally dislodged it with a blade of grass.

Morvenna sat with her hands over her eyes. 'No, I won't look,' she said. 'It's awful of you.'

But the ant was in the pit. She peered through the crack between her fingers and saw it. It looked big and strong, frenziedly pulling down the sand of the slope in its struggle to escape. Perhaps it might get away. She took down her hands and leant forward.

In their minds the ant and its arena of battle enlarged, filled the whole world. Under the sand at the pit-bottom crouched the lion, big as a real lion, waiting for the ant to slide down a little farther. But this one was so big; bigger than the ant-lion itself, Max said. 'Now we'll see some sport.'

The ant was puzzled at the sand that slipped so treacherously and persistently away as it climbed. It stopped, slid, went down almost to the bottom. For a moment there was a stir in the sand there, and Morvenna jumped. The ant might have seen it, too; at any rate it gathered all its strength and made a rush at the slope. The sand slid quickly but the ant was determined; he had almost reached the top. 'Good ant, good ant,' Morvenna cried; but Max pushed with his twig, and down went the ant to the bottom.

For a moment nothing happened. 'It's *too* big,' Max said, and his lips pursed. The two children stared down, lying on their stomachs, heads almost together. The ant hesitated and began to struggle up against the slope.

But now the ant-lion moved. Quick, dexterous, it thrust its stumpy forelegs from the sand and began to jerk its head, heavy and tool-like. Sand flew up, hindering the big ant, setting the walls slipping down. 'Ah,' Max breathed. 'Look at that now.'

The ant slipped and slipped, staying in the one place. It was growing tired, but it was clearly in a panic; its legs worked frantically. The hot shadows of the tree above moved across and across; the cicadas filled the afternoon with their monotonous shrill. The battle swayed. Morvenna moved aside; her rib was against a knotted root of the tree; and as she moved Max gave a shout of triumph. 'Oh, what happened?' She thrust him aside and peered down.

The ant-lion had seized the meat-ant by one leg. Those relentless tool-jaws hung on, like the jaws of a dingo harassing a sheep. The ant, caught at last, was putting out a desperate effort; his free legs thrashed wildly, he made a little headway, but the weight of the grub-like creature braced against him was too much, and he could find nothing to grip.

'I ought to save him,' Morvenna thought. 'I oughtn't to let . . . Mother would call it cruelty to animals.' But she no longer wanted to put down her twig, even if Max would let her. Shamed, enraptured, she clung to the tree-root with one hand and stared down.

The ant grew weaker, slower, his struggles more spasmodic. The lion saw his chance now; he released the leg and made for the ant's body, seizing him by the abdomen. There was a wild scurry in the pit now, the ant rearing in the fountaining sand. They could see those shovel-jaws working.

The silence was the strangest thing, Morvenna felt. Round them the afternoon continued; a wagtail hopped on the fence, other ants ran placidly about their business, the creek below made its endless liquid noise over the rocks; but to the two children all had shrunk to the dimensions of the pit, and the creatures in it, engaged in their soundless struggle, plunged and reared enormous. The golden air should have been full of their shrieks and groanings.

Now the ant fell. All was over; his waist almost severed, his legs quivering in the air, he lay helpless. How quickly, how ruthlessly, the ant-lion pulled him down avoiding the last kicks of those thin useless legs, touching him, severing abdomen from body, hiding him in the sand to serve for larder, where the other ants lay. The creature seemed like a little machine, a tool for some energy that possessed him; hideous, swift, he sent a shudder through Morvenna as she watched him.

Slowly, slowly the lion and his victim sank into the sand. Now they were only humps, sand-covered; now they had vanished. There lay the pit, still and innocent, its contours unchanged.

Max sat up slowly. His eyes looked large and dark.

'Are you going to put in another?' Morvenna asked. She half-hoped, half-feared it.

'No,' Max said. He stood up, not looking at the pit or at Morvenna. 'Enough's enough.'

'Are you going to bring Harry down and show it to him?' Morvenna persisted.

'Oh, shut up,' said Max. He stood uncertainly for a moment, detaching himself from the scene, from the afternoon, from Morvenna. Then he set off down the creek-bank, running faster and faster. Morvenna stood hesitating; then she too began to run. At last they stopped, far from the pit, exhausted and panting.

'What shall we do now?' Morvenna said.

JUDITH WRIGHT

6 | *Filling the gaps* *(Part 2)*

1 There are six missing words in the poem which follows. What do you think they might be?

First get a feel for the poem as a whole by reading it through twice. Then you can begin to jot down some words that might fit the gaps. (You may prefer to work on this activity in a small group.)

Remember, there are no 'right' answers here, although there will be some 'wrong' ones. What matters is whether your suggestions seem to fit, in terms of sound and meaning.

If you find it difficult to get started, list a few possible words for each gap. Then, after some thought, underline your favourite 'filler'.

2 When you have finished, compare your words with those chosen by other groups, and with the original poem which you will find on page 107.

Choose, out of all the versions, the words you like best and write out the full poem using them. You could add a suitable drawing.

The School Caretaker

In the corner of the playground
Down dark and slimy ▮A▮,
Lived a monster with a big nose
Full of curly hairs.

He had a bunch of keyrings
Carved out of little boys,
He confiscated ▮B▮
And all our favourite toys.

He wore a greasy ▮C▮,
Looked like an undertaker,
More scary than a horror film,
He was the school caretaker.

I left the school some years ago;
Saw him again the other day.
He looked rather sad and old
▮D▮ on his way.

It's funny when you grow up
How grown-ups start growing down,
And the ▮E▮ upon their faces
Are no more than a frown.

In the corner of the playground
Down dark and slimy stairs,
Sits a ▮F▮ little man
With a nose full of curly hairs.

7 | *Making the spaces*

Now take a look at this poem by Shel Silverstein. In small groups or by yourself, read the poem aloud several times.

Think back to the 'filling the gaps' approach you used on page 27. This time, you are going to decide which words should be blanked out to create the 'gaps'.

1 If you were asked to blank out six words that would be very easy to guess, which would they be?

2 If you had to choose the six most difficult words to guess, when blanked out, what might they be? (Start by listing a number of possible words, then, after some thought, decide on the 'best' six words to turn into gaps.)

3 Copy out your 'easy' and 'difficult' versions and see how they compare with those produced by other groups.

UNSCRATCHABLE ITCH

There is a spot that you can't scratch
Right between your shoulder blades,
Like an egg that just won't hatch
Here you set and there it stays.
Turn and squirm and try to reach it,
Twist your neck and bend your back,
Hear your elbows creak and crack,
Stretch your fingers, now you bet it's
Going to reach—no that won't get it—
Hold your breath and stretch and pray,
Only just an inch away,
Worse than a sunbeam you can't catch
Is that one spot that
You can't scratch.

Follow on . . .

Using your two versions, you can now carry out your own experiment on as many people as you can persuade to help you. Show each person *either* the 'easy' *or* the 'difficult' version, and ask them to guess the words which you have blanked out. Keep a note of their correct guesses.

Then write up your findings and discover just how successful your two versions were.

Diagrams like these will help you to make more sense of your results:

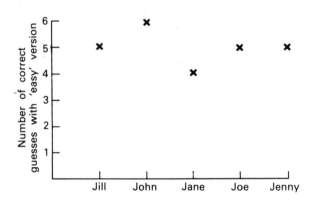

1 How successful were you?

2 Was your 'easy' version as easy as you thought?

3 Was your 'difficult' version as difficult as you expected?

4 What conclusions can you draw from your findings?

5 Knowing what you know now, do you wish to make any changes to either version?

6 If you do, which changes would you make and why?

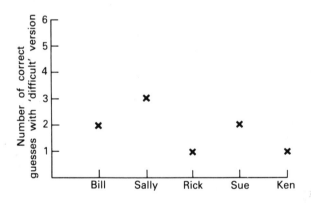

What comes next? *(Episode 2)*

Second Impressions

Here is Episode 2.

The ship entered Earth's atmosphere. Its metal skin now drove against air instead of nothingness. The ship screamed. Its metal skin changed colour and in places glowed dull red with the heat.

F The In-Flight Tech's cocoon shifted, tearing from its framing. A cluster of tiny tubes pulled away from a socket, away from the needle. Blood, drugs squirted uselessly. The In-Flight Tech died without a word.

The Captain watched his light go out and said, 'All right. All right. Alone. I'll do it alone.'

* * *

They stopped their wrestling match and looked about them.

G 'You heard it! It went sort of wheeoosh,' Kevin said to Reg. 'Wheeeeeooooosh.' Reg flicked his head sideways to acknowledge his master's words, but went on staring at the dark corner of the trees. Reg had heard the noise. He didn't know where it came from, but he knew where it led. He marked the place in his nose and mind. Over there, by the dark trees.

* * *

'So that's what it's like,' said the Captain. He had never before experienced a smash landing. He had to say something, even if there was no one to hear him. He kept his voice level.

He waited for the needle to deliver whatever his body needed. While he waited, he disciplined his mind and made it think and plan.

H 'Conquest,' this mind said. 'I am alone, but I am still here as a conqueror. I will conquer this planet.'

'Method,' he continued. 'I am alone; but usual procedure will be followed. I will find a creature of the planet. I will invade its mind: make it obey me. I will then make all creatures of its kind obey the creature I inhabit.'

'Having conquered one creature and one species, I will move on, always seeking the higher creatures. If there is a ruling species on this planet, I will invade a creature of that species and thus become ruler of all.'

He pressed the Release Control. The halves of the cocoon opened.

The new conqueror of the planet Earth flexed his limbs, tested his organs and senses, opened the main doors and stepped forth.

* * *

I Kevin pretended not to hear his mother's call, but then decided to obey. A long way away, right at the edge of the field, he could see the yellow glimmer of the lamp on her bicycle. 'Oh lor,' he thought, 'she's had to get on the bike to come after me. She won't be pleased. . . .' To the dog, he said, 'Come on, Reg. Come on, boy!' But Reg was running back and forth by the dark trees.

To start you thinking:

- 1 How many survived the crash?

- 2 What was it that Kevin and Reg heard?

- 3 (a) What do you feel when you read the sentence 'Over there, by the dark trees' (section G)?
  (b) Which is the important word here?
  (c) Why?

- 4 From the clues you have been given, what sort of a man do you think the Captain is?

- 5 What might Kevin say to his mother (section I)?

- 6 What is Reg up to (section I)?

- 7 Now make your own notes about this episode. Remember the headings:

* Things you liked
* Things you disliked
* Things that interested you
* Things that surprised you
* Things that confused you
* What might happen next?
* Any other thoughts?

Whirling words

Often, words or phrases can taken on several different meanings, depending on how they are being used. As you read the story on the next page, look for as many different meanings as you can.

When you have read the story, **answer the following questions** in small groups.

1   Make a list of all the words or phrases with double meanings that you can find in the story (for example, 'a bit of a jam').

2   Add six words or phrases of your own to this list — words or phrases which are also capable of being understood in different ways. You may need to give some examples to make the different meanings clear. For example: those 'green fingers' successful gardeners have; feeling 'down in the dumps' when miserable; or 'over the moon' when very happy.

3   (a) Compared your list with those from other groups.
    (b) Are there any words or phrases which seem to be class favourites?

Follow on . . .

- 1   At the end of the story, Francis, Sarah and Mr Delmonico arrive home, 'but the whirling words are still with us'.
     Continue the story, using the 'whirling words' idea, until the spell is finally broken.

- 2   Words and phrases with double meanings are often used in jokes. For example:

    Q   How can you keep cool at a football match?

    A   *Stand next to a fan.*

Q   Why do golfers take an extra pair of trousers with them?

A   *In case they get a hole in one.*

Write down at least two other jokes like these.

Trouble in the Supermarket
Margaret Mahy

One day when he was in a very joking mood Mr Delmonico offended a word witch. He did it by being a bit too clever. (Too much cleverness is often offensive to witches.)

Mr Delmonico, with his twins, Francis and Sarah, was shopping at the supermarket. The witch was there too, pushing a shopping trolley and talking to herself as word witches do ... they need a lot of words going on around them all the time.

'I'll have some peanut butter,' she said.

'You'd butter not,' cried Mr Delmonico, laughing at his own joke. The word witch took no notice, just went on talking to herself.

'And then perhaps I'll have a loaf of wholemeal bread,' she went on.

Mr Delmonico winked at the twins. 'How can you make a meal out of a hole?' he asked. 'It doesn't sound very nice.'

Francis and Sarah were horrified to hear their father speaking so carelessly to a word witch. But the witch ignored him. She was trying hard to behave well in a public place.

'I'll get some beans,' she muttered.

Mr Delmonico looked at the beans. He couldn't resist another joke. 'They look more like "might-have-beans",' he remarked with a smile.

Now the witch turned on him, glaring with her small red eyes. 'I've had quite enough of you,' she cried. 'You shall suffer whirling words and see how you like it.'

Mr Delmonico was suddenly serious as the word witch scuttled away.

Whirling words sounded as if they might be painful.

'I'm afraid I might have got us into a bit of a jam,' he said to the twins.

'Daddy, be careful,' cried Sarah, but it was too late. They were up to their ankles in several kinds of jam. Francis was mainly mixed up with strawberry, Sarah with plum and apple, while Mr Delmonico himself had melon and ginger jam up over the turn-ups of his trousers. The manager of the supermarket came hurrying up.

'What's going on here?' he cried.

'Nothing really,' Mr Delmonico said, trying to sound casual. 'Just some jam that was lying around.'

'There's something fishy about this,' declared the manager and then gasped, for a large flapping fish appeared out of nowhere and struck him on the right ear. Sarah and Francis realized that anyone near Mr Delmonico was going to suffer from whirling words too.

'You are to blame for all this mess,' said the manager, 'and you'll have to pay for it.'

'Oh, will I?' replied Mr Delmonico, trying hard to keep calm. 'Wait till I ring my lawyer.'

An elegant gold ring with an enormous diamond in it appeared in his hand. Mr Delmonico looked guilty and tried to hide it behind the bottles of vinegar. 'You can do what you like, you'll have to pay,' said the manager.

'Me? *Pay?* Look at my trousers all over jam! I shall lose my temper in a moment. You're just egging me on.'

Eggs began to fall out of the air. A few of them hit the supermarket manager, but most of them broke on Mr Delmonico. He was jam to the knees and egg to the ears.

'Stop it!' cried the manager. 'And you talk of lawyers — why, you haven't got a leg to stand on.'

Mr Delmonico sat down suddenly in the jam.

'We must get out of this before the balloon goes up,' whispered Francis to Sarah, and he found himself rising out of the jam, Sarah beside him. To their delight a beautiful air balloon was carrying them gently away.

'Quick!' said Francis. 'Grab Dad.'

Catching Mr Delmonico by the collar and by the belt of his trousers his clever twins hoisted him into the air.

The manager waved his fist at them and shouted: 'You haven't heard the last of this.'

The balloon swooped through the supermarket door and skimmed over the roofs of the town.

'Home!' ordered Mr Delmonico. 'I'm not going to *that* shop again. They have a very funny way of displaying fish and jam.'

Francis shook his head. 'You shouldn't have teased the word witch, Dad.'

'Oh, these word witches need to be teased,' Mr Delmonico replied grandly, 'wispy creatures with their heads in the clouds — whereas I am a pretty down to earth fellow.'

At that moment Mr Delmonico's collar and trouser belt gave way and he fell to earth — fortunately into his very own garden which he had dug and raked that morning until it was as soft as velvet.

'We're home,' said Francis, 'but the whirling words are still with us. What will we do about that?'

Sometimes it is only possible to make sense of a poem by attempting to read it aloud, especially when it is written in a local dialect.

Barry Heath comes from a part of the East Midlands that is a mixture of Derbyshire, South Yorkshire and Nottinghamshire. He has tried to write his poem as he would read it.

1 First read this poem to yourself a couple of times.

2 Then write out, in 'ordinary' English, the first three lines of the third verse:
wistopped ahtside this
misers ahhs an ah
knocked ont doower

3 In small groups, take turns to read the poem aloud — trying to read it as Barry Heath might read it. Then decide which is the best way to read it and why

4 Now write the whole poem out as a BBC newsreader might read it, in 'ordinary' English. You might have to add extra words (for example, a word is missing in the first line), or even change some words all together.

5 Which version do you think is more effective — the poem as it was written by Barry Heath, or the 'translation' written in 'ordinary' English? Give reasons for your answer.

Follow on . . .

Now try to write your own poem in your local dialect. Try out some ideas in rough first and say it aloud to yourself to get just the right sounds.

GUY FAWKES

we wantud best Guy Fawkes
on ower street
so widressed ower lez
up
wipurra stick upiz back
a stick up each sleeve
one up each trahser
leg
an purrim in a barra

along Crown street
up Richo an dahn
Big Barn Lane,
thed neva seen owt
like it
rait prahd wewus
weus pockets jinglin
an lez stiff as a
cork

wistopped ahtside this
misers ahhs an ah
knocked ont doower
'Penny fut guy mista!'
ah shahtud t'misruble
sod
an ee cum aht wavin
a big axe an ah
run

Lez cuddunt run cos
ee warrin barra
so wileft im
'ah'll geeya blewdy
guy' shahtud miser
an went t'chop it up
un lez jumped aht
fraitenin miser t'
death

miser dropt axe
anrun up path
an ower lez run
stiffleggud dahnt
lane shahtin 'Wayit
f'me! Wayit f'me!'

Words into pictures

The short story by Anne Cameron on the following pages lends itself well to a comic strip style of telling. But to do this you will have to simplify everything, especially the speech. Read the story carefully first.

1 Break the story up into its most important moments or episodes, and write down what happens in each. A story like 'My Very Strange Teeth' will probably have four or five episodes within it. Each episode can be given a whole page in your comic strip version.

2 Then decide which words *need* to be spoken. Write them down, but use as little talk as possible — let your choice of pictures tell the story for you.

3 Do not worry too much about the quality of your drawing — matchstick people work well. The secret is to be bold and try to make your comic strip look interesting by varying what is seen in the frames. Go for close-ups in some, long distance shots in others. Keep ringing the changes.

Here is a possible 'first page' to get you started. But your version does not have to have the same number of frames per page. Experiment with your layout in rough. Take risks! (For more help on how to make comics turn to 'Professor Mindboggle' on page 44.)

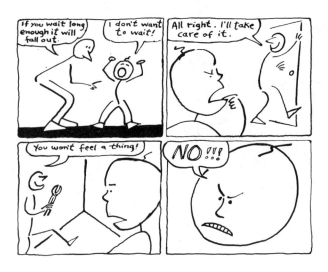

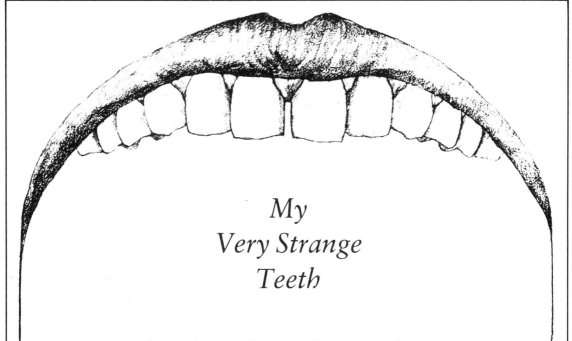

My
Very Strange
Teeth

My mother and Huey were listening. My father and I were talking.

"Well," my father said, "if you wait long enough, it will fall out." He was talking about my tooth, my right bottom front tooth.

"How long do I have to wait?" I asked. Because I had *two* right bottom front teeth – one firm little new one pushing in, and one wiggly old one.

"I can't say," my father said. "Maybe a month, maybe two months. Maybe less."

"I don't want to wait," I said. "I want *one* tooth there, and I don't want to wait two months!"

"All right!" said my father. "I'll take care of it!" He jumped out of his chair and ran out of the door to the garage. He was back in a minute, carrying something – a pair of pliers!

"Your tooth is a little loose already," my father said. "So I'll just put the pliers in your mouth for a second, twist, and the tooth will come out. You won't feel a thing!"

"I won't feel a thing?" I looked at the pliers – huge, black-handled pliers with a long pointed tip. I thought I *would* feel a thing. I thought it would hurt.

"Shall I?" said my dad. He raised the pliers towards my mouth.

"NO!" I said. "Not that way! Don't you know any other way to take out a tooth?"

"Well," he answered, "when I was a boy the main way was with a pair of pliers – but there was another way. Just you wait."

He jumped up again and ran to the cupboard. When he came back, he had a spool of black thread. Thread didn't look as painful as pliers.

"This is a simple way," my father said. "Just let me tie this thread around your old tooth."

"All right," I said.

Very carefully my father tied the end of the thread around my old tooth. That didn't hurt.

"Now," my father said, "stand here by the door."

I stood by the kitchen door, and my father tied the other end of the thread to the doorknob.

"Now what?" I said.

"Now," my father said, "you just close your eyes . . ."

"What are you going to do?" I asked. I wasn't

going to close my eyes when I didn't know what was happening.

"This is a *good* method from the old days," my father said. "You close your eyes. Then – very suddenly – I shove the kitchen door shut. Snap! The thread pulls the tooth right out!"

I looked at the kitchen door. It was a lot bigger than I was – and about 20 million times bigger than my tooth.

"Won't it – hurt?" I was really afraid I might lose my whole head with the tooth.

"Oh, just a little," my father said. "Just for a *second*."

"No thanks," I said. "Please take this thread off my tooth!"

"All right then." My father shrugged his shoulders and took the string off my tooth.

"Don't you know *any other* way?"

"There is one other way," my father said. "Go into the bathroom, stand over the sink, and just keep pushing the tooth with your finger till it comes out."

"Will that hurt?"

"You can stop pushing when it hurts," my father said. "Of course it takes longer – I would be very glad to do it with either the pliers or the doorknob."

"No thanks," I said. I started pushing on my tooth with my finger. "Why can't I push it out here?" I asked. "Why do I have to do it over the sink?"

"When you get the tooth out," my father said, "it'll bleed. That's why you take the tooth out over the sink – so you have cold water to rinse your mouth and stop the bleeding."

"*How much* bleeding?"

"Some. Enough so you should use the sink."

I decided right then that my old tooth could stay in my mouth right beside the new one as long as it wanted – two months, two years, any time.

"I've changed my mind," I said. "That tooth can stay, even if it is stupid to have two teeth where one should be."

"It's not stupid," my mother said, "just unusual. You have very special teeth. I bet prehistoric cavemen would have liked to have your teeth."

"Why?"

"They ate a lot of raw meat," my mother said. "It must have been hard for a cave boy to eat raw meat with teeth missing. But you have two teeth in the space of one. You could have eaten mastodon meat or sabre-toothed tiger meat, or anything the hunters brought home."

A cave boy with two teeth in place of one. I wished I had a time machine to go back to the *very* old days – before pliers and before door-knobs – back to the caves. I curled my lower lip under.

"You look like a cave boy," my mother said.

"You should show the kids at school your teeth," Huey said.

"Maybe I will," I said.

I went to my room and made a sign for myself. It read –

```
See Cave-Boy Teeth
      one pence
1p              1p
```

I wore the sign at break the next day.

My friends came around. "What does *that* mean?" they asked.

"Uh. Uh." I grunted and held up a penny. I couldn't explain. If I talked, they'd see my teeth for free.

After a while one girl gave me a penny, and I showed her my special cave-boy teeth. Some of the other kids had missing teeth, but nobody had two teeth in one space like mine.

I ran all the way home after school to tell my mother what had happened. I said, "Tomorrow I'll show more kids!"

I picked up an apple that lay on the kitchen table and took a big bite.

"Ow!" I said, because I could feel my old tooth twist in my mouth. In a minute, without too much blood, it was lying on my hand. "OW!" I said again, not because it hurt, but because right then was the end of my special, mastodon-eating, double-biting, cave-boy teeth.

THE WORDS THAT PEOPLE SAY IN COMIC BOOKS ARE PUT INSIDE SHAPES CALLED *BALLOONS!*

IT'S A GOOD IDEA TO WRITE THE WORDS FIRST AND THEN PUT THE BALLOON AROUND THEM!

IF YOU DRAW THE BALLOON FIRST, YOU MIGHT RUN OUT OF SPACE!

THE REALLY *IMPORTANT* WORDS INSIDE BALLOONS ARE SOMETIMES *BIGGER* THAN OTHERS!

DO YOU KNOW HOW TO MAKE A BALLOON THAT SHOWS WHAT SOMEBODY IS THINKING?

YES!

LIKE THIS!

PROFESSOR MINDBOGGLE IS LOSING HIS HAIR!

IN THE CELLAR...

NOT ALL WORDS IN COMICS ARE IN BALLOONS!

LOOK OUT, PROFESSOR!

LIKE WHEN YOU WANT SOMETHING TO MAKE A NOISE!

BONK!

BESIDES WORDS, COMICS USE *SYMBOLS*... FOR INSTANCE, TO SHOW THAT SOMEONE IS HURT!

...OR PUZZLED!

... OR ANGRY!

Now choose another short story and re-tell it as a comic strip. You could use a story you have written yourself, something you have read recently or even borrow an idea from television. Anything that makes you think in pictures. If you cannot find anything suitable, try a comic strip based on this story outline:

The Pullover

David's gran gave him a pullover with flowers on.

He hated it.

He 'lost' it — his parents always found it.

He left it in the garden — the dog always brought it in.

He put it in the washing machine on 'Hot' — it would not shrink.

When out walking one day. . .

He found a loose thread in the sleeve — he pulled it.

A crow swooped down — it grabbed the end of the thread.

The crow flew into a tree — it wound the pullover off David.

It made a nest.

The next day David showed his gran the nest.

12 | *What comes next?* *(Episode 3)*

Third Impressions

Here is Episode 3.

'Keeeevin!' his mother shouted. 'You come home now, or I'll –'

'It's Reg. HE won't come!' shouted Kevin furiously.

J And he wouldn't. Kevin could see Reg running up and down, doing a sort of sentry duty on the trot by the edge of the trees. The dog's ears were pricked, his tail was high, his body alert. He wouldn't obey.

* * *

The Captain's helmet indicators read S A F E, so the planet's air was breathable. Nevertheless, he kept his helmet on. He was glad to be protected with-helmet and armour. He was grateful to the brains and skills that had designed his armoured suit and given him a strength greater than his own. The Captain could clench a hand — and the suit's own metal hand would clench with such force that it could crush metal. The Captain was strong and fit — but his suit was tireless and inexhaustible. If the Captain's nerves, muscles and movements said 'run', the suit would run endlessly. If the Captain's body said 'climb', the suit would keep climbing for him.

Now was the time, the Captain realized, to climb.

K He had seen many worlds, explored many planets. He had never seen one like this. This world was bursting with life. From the corner of his eye, the Captain saw something move, very fast, on several legs. Above him, something flew. Behind him, something scurried. He was not in the least surprised. How could there fail to be active, animal life in so rich a place?

Climbing was what mattered now. He had to get on and up. Where he stood, he was completely surrounded and blinded by vegetable richness. Great green ribbed things, taller than the highest mountains of his own planet, reached indefinitely upwards — no, not indefinitely, he could see dark blue sky still further above. A vast green trunk sprang from the soil very near him. It was the right size and shape and it had projections: ideal for climbing. He clasped his limbs round this trunk. The suit took over and climbed him towards the dark blue sky, away from the ship with its hideous cargo of broken bodies, and from the stench of death.

* * *

At first, there had just been a faint whiff of it. Now, it was a full-bodied and glorious stench — better still, a new stench! Reg's black nostrils widened still further. There! Over there! He gave a stifled yelp of ecstasy as the smell strengthened; he bounded towards it.

L 'Kevin!' said his mother. 'Never mind the dog, you come home and eat your supper. Come on, now! I'm not waiting a moment longer!'

Kevin stopped and gave one last yell. 'Reg! Reeeeeg!'

Reg did not hear. Only tracking down the smell mattered.

*   *   *

The Captain could climb no higher. The green column that supported him was bending and swaying under his weight. He wrapped his limbs round the column and felt the suit lock itself securely into position. He looked around him.

He was in a dense forest of green columns, all very much the same as the one he had climbed yet each different. A few were red-like (his column was ribbed and almost flat). Some columns carried grotesque explosions of strange branching shapes on their heads. A great nest of columns in the distance supported flat, outward-branching green platforms and — amazing! — complicated crown-shaped yellow platforms at their summits.

M He adjusted his helmet to take in air from the outside. The air was moist, perfumed, sumptuous. He let the helmet supply his mouth with a sample of the moisture that was making droplets over everything; the water was cold, clean, simple, almost certainly safe — and absolutely delicious. On his own planet, he had tasted such air and water only in the laboratories. Reluctantly, he returned to the closed-circuit environment of his suit and helmet. . . .

An amazing planet! A planet of limitless, unending, inexhaustible richness! And he was to be its conqueror. The thought was stunning. For once, the Captain allowed himself simply to feel pleasure: to stare at nothing and to dream of glory.

To start you thinking:

- 1 What is so unusual about the dog's behaviour (section J)?

- 2 What do you think the Captain saw 'from the corner of his eye' (section K)?

- 3 What do you think could be the new smell in Reg's nostrils (section L)?

- 4 What is it that the Captain seems to be climbing (sections K and L)?

- 5 Now make your own notes about this episode. Remember the headings:

  * Things you liked
  * Things you disliked
  * Things that interested you
  * Things that surprised you
  * Things that confused you
  * What might happen next?
  * Any other thoughts?

Read this poem several times.

Can you think of a solution to the puzzle? One way forward would be if friend *one* (the person who wrote the poem), wrote a letter to friend *two* (the one going about with Tracy Hackett). The letter would explain exactly what she thought was going on between them all. Friend two would then reply, putting her side of the picture. They could then both take it from there!

1   (a) What might those two letters say? Write them both, as if they were real pieces of correspondence.
      or
  (b) Imagine that this poem is a letter to the 'Problem page' of a magazine. What would your reply be? Write your reply as it would appear in the magazine.

Follow on . . .

- 1   (a) Now that you have worked on the poem a little, explain how you know that the speaking voice (*my* friend, *I* would like to get her back) is a girl? What is there in the poem which leads you to that conclusion? Give some examples to back up your arguments.
  (b) Would it make any difference to the poem if the speaking voice was a boy? Give reasons for your answer.
  (c) Try re-writing the poem with a boy as the main speaking voice. What other changes would you need to make and why?

- 2 Misunderstanding between friends can often cause difficulties. After sharing some examples in a small group, write about a time when just such a misunderstanding upset a friendship that you valued. Write about your experience either as a poem or as a short story.

It is a Puzzle

My friend
Is not my friend anymore.
She has secrets from me
And goes about with Tracy Hackett.

I would
Like to get her back,
Only do not want to say so.
So I pretend
To have secrets from her
And go about with Alice Banks.

But what bothers me is,
Maybe *she* is pretending
And would like *me* back,
Only does not want to say so.

On the other hand,
How can we be friends
And have secrets from each other
And go about with other people?

In which case
Maybe it bothers her
That *I* am pretending.

My friend
Is not my friend anymore,
Unless she is pretending.
I cannot think what to do.
It is a puzzle.

But if we are both pretending,
Then really we are friends
And do not know it.

14 | *First impressions* (2)

On the next page is the first chapter of a book called *The Computer Nut* by the American writer Betsy Byars.

Writers always try to make opening chapters interesting, so that their readers will want to continue with the book. However, in this case you can't continue reading so you will have to do the next best thing and continue the story yourself. But before you start writing, answer questions 1–7.

1 (a) What sort of job does Kate's father have?
   (b) There are at least three clues that will help you here. What are they?
   (c) How do they help?

2 (a) Who is 'Miss Markham'?
   (b) Give reasons for your answer.

3 List all the 'American' words used in the chapter and explain what you think each one means.

4 From the way Kate talks and behaves, how old do you think she is? Give reasons for your choice.

5 (a) What picture do we get of Willie Lomax?
   (b) How do you see him?

6 (a) Do you think Kate likes Willie Lomax?
   (b) Give reasons for your answer.

7 The writer has decided to end the chapter with the idea that something interesting might happen 'tomorrow'. How would you continue the story? Will Kate immediately return to her father's office? Or will other things happen?

8 Now, bearing in mind what you already know about Kate, her father, Miss Markham and Willie Lomax, continue the story in a way that is interesting to you.

Follow on . . .

When you have finished your story, borrow a copy of *The Computer Nut* from a library. Read it through, then write a short review of the whole book, concentrating on the *differences* between the original story and your version.

Say which bits you like best from each version.

Self-Portrait of a Computer Nut

Kate was drawing a picture of herself on her father's computer. She had been working for an hour. She was half finished when Miss Markham came and stood in the doorway behind her.

"I'm ready to close the office now, Kate," she said.

Kate flicked her hair behind her ears. She did not answer. She continued to turn the thumbwheels, drawing lines between the dots. Her eyes watched the screen intently.

"Kate, did you hear me? The last patient has left. Your father has gone to the hospital. I'm ready to close the office now."

"Go ahead. I'll lock the doors when I leave."

"You know that's against your father's orders."

"Well, I've *got* to finish this. It's homework and it's due tomorrow."

"Katie—"

"Miss Markham, this is the first art assignment I've ever been interested in. Last week you know what we did? We made Indian signs out of yarn, and before that we pasted macaroni on cardboard. Now, *finally*, we are doing something I'm interested in, and I've got to finish."

Miss Markham crossed the room and stood behind Kate. She watched the screen as Kate connected the dots for her mouth. "That does *not* look like homework."

"It is! Our assignment is to do a self-portrait."

"On a computer?"

"No. We're supposed to use our imaginations. Willie Lomax is doing a collage out of candy wrappers. His freckles are M & M's. He's calling it Sweet Freak."

"What are you calling yours?"

"Self-Portrait of a Computer Nut."

"Good title."

"I like it." Kate smiled without glancing around.

Miss Markham watched as Kate drew circles in her eyes. She sighed. "All right, Kate, you can keep working until I change out of my uniform."

"Thanks."

"But then you have *got* to leave whether you're through or not."

"I'll be through."

As Miss Markham started for the door, she added, "If you're not, you'll have to call it 'Unfinished Portrait of a Computer Nut'. Ten minutes, Kate."

"Right."

With her eyes watching the screen, Kate drew the straight lines for her hair. She paused to look at what she'd done. "Not bad." She typed "Self-Portrait of a

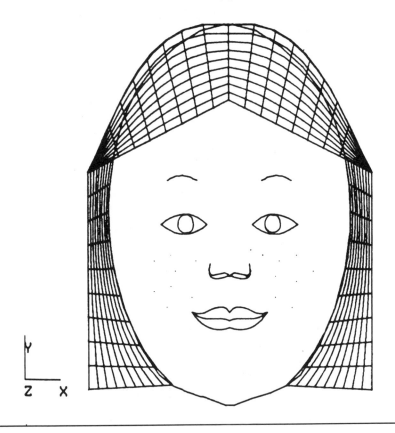

Computer Nut" beneath the picture. Then she pushed the button marked "Hard Copy" and waited while the machine printed the picture.

When the sheet of paper slid out of the side, Kate picked it up. "That does look like me," she said to herself.

She turned to shut off the computer and saw Miss Markham in the doorway. "Perfect timing," Kate said. She held up her picture. "What do you think?"

"Not bad. Your hair's never that neat, though."

"I know, and I also have more freckles, and braces on my teeth."

She eyed the sheet of paper critically. "Well, it's better than Willie's candy portrait. You know what happened last summer? I meant to tell you this. Willie went to the same computer camp as I did, and when we were checking in, his suitcase fell open, and there was a real thin layer of clothes—one T-shirt and a pair of socks—and the whole rest of the suitcase was junk food. He had enough Snickers to—"

"Kate, I have not got time to talk about Willie Lomax."

"I don't want to talk about him either!" Kate said quickly. She turned back to the computer to hide her expression. "I just wanted you to know that next time he's in for a checkup do not believe him when he says he has stuck to his diet."

Kate slipped out the disk containing the drawing program. To change the subject, she said, "Where are you going, Miss Markham? Do you have a date?"

"Not unless I leave right this minute."

"I'm coming! I'm coming!"

Kate was reaching for the off button when suddenly words began appearing on the screen. She stopped, her hand frozen in midair.

"That's crazy!"

She glanced at the door to see if Miss Markham had

noticed, but Miss Markham was in the outer office, turning off the lights. Kate sank into the chair, her portrait forgotten in her lap.

The words on the screen were:

I HAVE JUST SEEN THE PORTRAIT OF THE
COMPUTER NUT AND I WOULD LIKE TO MAKE
CONTACT. WILL YOU RECEIVE A MESSAGE,
COMPUTER NUT?

Kate read the words a second time. A flutter of excitement moved up her spine. "Miss Markham, could you please come in here?" she called. "I want you to see this. It's weird."

"I am ready to leave, Kate. I am standing by the door with my coat on. My hand is on the doorknob."

"Has this computer been acting funny lately?"

"I am opening the door, Kate."

"Wait! It's happening again!"

REPEAT. I HAVE A MESSAGE FOR THE
COMPUTER NUT. WILL YOU RECEIVE? INPUT
YES OR NO.

"I am stepping outside, Kate."

"Miss Markham, somebody is sending me a message. I cannot believe this. On the computer! Somebody saw my portrait and they're sending me a message."

"I am closing the door, Kate."

"Wait! Let me get my message! I—Oh, all right! I'm coming!"

Hurriedly Kate put her hands on the keyboard and typed one word:

TOMORROW.

Then she got to her feet and turned off the computer. The screen dimmed and, holding her self-portrait in one hand, she ran for the door.

One thing leading to another

When we read stories, we often find that one incident or event leads directly on to another — the story gradually builds up, step by step by step. As readers, we might be half expecting some steps; but at other times, stories come as a series of shocks or surprises.

'News' is a step-by-step story which goes from 'bad' to 'worse' through a series of unexpected shocks.

By yourself, or in small groups, read the story through carefully.

News

A rich landowner was returning home from a journey when he met by the side of the road the steward he had left in charge of his estate while he was away.

'Ah, steward,' hailed the returning gentleman cheerily, 'how are you, old fellow? And how are things at home?'

'Bad enough, sir,' said the steward. 'The magpie is dead.'

'Well, well,' said the gentleman. 'Poor magpie. Gone at last, eh? And how did he die?'

'Over-ate himself, sir.'

'Did he indeed! The greedy bird! What was it he liked so much?'

'Horseflesh. That's what got him, sir. Horseflesh.'

'Never!' said the landowner. 'How ever did he manage to find so much horseflesh that it killed him?'

'All your father's horses, sir.'

'What! My father's horses! Are they dead too?'

'Aye, sir. Died of overwork.'

'Why ever should they be overworked, steward?'

'Carrying all that water, sir.'

'Carrying water! What were they carrying water for, man?'

'For sure, sir, to put the fire out.'

'Fire! What fire?'

'Why, sir, the fire that burned your father's house to the ground.'

'Good Lord, steward, is my father's house burnt down? How did that happen?'

'I reckon it were the torches, sir.'

'What torches?'

'Them we used at your mother's funeral, sir.'

'My mother is dead?'

'Aye, poor lady. She never looked up after it.'

'After what, man, after what?'

'The loss of your father, sir.'

'My father? Dead too?'

'Yes, poor gentleman. Took to his bed as soon as he heard of it.'

'Heard of what?'

'Of the bad news, sir.'

'More bad news! What bad news?'

'Well, sir, your bank has failed and all your money is lost, and you're not worth a penny in the world, sir. I thought I'd come and wait on you to tell you about it, sir, for I thought you'd like to hear the news.'

1   Pick out the items of bad news the steward tells the returning gentleman. Draw a 'stepping stone' chart like this:

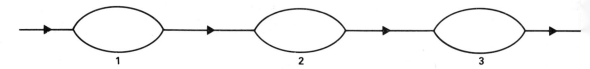

For each step, write down one of the items of bad news. For example, on the first step, simply write: 'Death of magpie'. Then move on to step two and the next item, and so on and so on, until you reach the end of the story.

2   How many steps were there all together?

Follow on . . .

Write your own story, 'More News', where, once again, one piece of bad news leads on to something even worse.

You will need to try out your story in rough first, perhaps using a 'stepping stone' chart. Group discussion might also help you to plan your work.

Fourth impressions

Here is Episode 4.

N HERE! Reg's nose was actually touching the wonderful source of the supreme stench! He licked the source of the smell. It was cold and dewy and hard. He had expected something still warm, still half alive, still rubbery-soft; it was that sort of smell. But perhaps the cold, hard outer case was only a container, like the tube of bone that encloses the marrow? Carefully, he opened his mouth and picked up the container thing in his jaws. Nothing happened, so he put it down again, holding it between his front paws, and looked at it with his head on one side.

It seemed harmless. He lowered his head, opened his jaws and bit.

* * *

O The Captain saw a monster.

Once the terror and shock were over there were three things to be done (Past, Present and Future, as the training manuals put it). First, understand exactly what had happened — the Past; second, make up your mind what immediate action to take — Present; third, decide what advantage could be gained by further action — Future.

All right. Past. He had seen the monster — a living thing, not a machine — travel at incredible speed, crash through the green columns and spires, trampling them flat in its haste. The monster was white, brown and black and ran on legs. It had made straight for the crashed ship. When the monster's face opened, it was pink inside and had pointed white mountains above and below.

The monster had done various things, that the Captain could not see, to the ship. Finally it had picked up the ship, holding it between the white mountains, and crushed it. The Captain had heard the metal screech.

All right. Now the Present.

The body of the monster must be entered by the Captain so that the Captain could take it over in the usual way. He had to get nearer the monster. That should be easy enough provided that the monster did not suddenly go away on its big legs.

Finally, the Future.

Well, that was obvious enough, thought the Captain. Follow the normal procedure. Invade the monster's brain and gain control of its body and its actions.

After that, the invasion would follow its normal course. All species — high or low — would eventually obey the Captain. By then the Captain would have contacted his

What comes next?

home planet. More ships would come bearing settlers. At last the Captain's race would have found a safe, fitting, rich and permanent home.

He went towards the monster.

To start you thinking:

The different threads of the story should be coming together now.

1 What was that 'container thing' that Reg picked up in his jaws (section N)?

2 Who, or what, is the 'monster'?

3 The Captain seems to have worked out a plan to 'take over' the 'monster'. Describe, in your own words, the Captain's plan.

4 (a) What are your feelings for the Captain at this point in the story?
   (b) Have they changed from how you felt after reading Episode 2?
   (c) In what ways?

5 Now make your own notes about this episode. Remember the headings:

* Things you liked
* Things you disliked
* Things that interested you
* Things that surprised you
* Things that confused you
* What might happen next?
* Any other thoughts?

One-sided conversation

Read through this 'conversation' piece carefully.

Watch with Father

Son, I don't care a row of beans whether it is your favourite programme or not. You are not watching it and that is the end of the matter.

Because it is a load of old codswallop, that's why not.

What Spotty Gleason's father lets him do is irrelevant to your case. If Spotty Gleason's father wants to see Spotty Gleason turned into a shambling moron before his very eyes, that is entirely a matter for him.

Anyway, you watch too much television.

Don't argue the toss with me, lad! You are glued to that set from the minute you get home till the minute you go to bed.

Oh, yes you are! Take last night as a typical example. At half-past seven, you were sitting there with a congealed fried-egg sandwich in your fist, you'd been watching non-stop for three hours and you were still wearing your cap and raincoat.

And another thing. Next time you come down for a glass of water you drink the glass of water and go straight to bed. You do not hang about at the back of the room gawping at 'Police Five', 'News at Ten', 'Upstairs, Downstairs', 'The Frost Programme' and 'Science and Religion'.

I have told you already, Spotty Gleason's leisure activities do not concern me in any degree whatever. You will be telling me next that Spotty Gleason stays up for the late night horror movie.

He does, does he? Well you're not going to, I can assure you of that. You do realise that you've got black rings under your eyes, don't you? Eight years old and you look like a blessed panda.

I have not the slightest intention of buying a bigger set. The only remaining decision to be made about T.V. sets in this household is whether the present one goes in the dustbin or not.

And I'll tell you something else for nothing while we're on the subject. When this round-the-clock lark starts up, I don't want to find you watching the thing at eight o'clock in the morning.

Because I say so.

You would think it a good enough explanation if I were to accompany it with a clout over the head, I do promise you.

Oh, very well, then, if you've got to have a reason for everything. Because it's not natural, that's why not.

Because it isn't.

Because I say so.

Look son, let's get this thing in perspective. Television is just another invention like radio or the motor car. It is intended to be the servant and not the master of humanity. This means that we shall not be watching it during the daylight hours.

The fact that I drive the car in the mornings has nothing to do with it. What I am saying is that it's one thing to watch the telly in the evenings, within reason when the day's work is finished. It is quite another thing to sit boggle eyed in front of it at breakfast time when the day's work hasn't even started.

I don't care what they do in America, or what Spotty Gleason plans to do in the United Kingdom. If you think that you are going to squat in front of that set scooping cornflakes into your face while they re-run last night's "Opportunity Knocks" you are sadly mistaken.

I have never denied that I listen to the radio while shaving. That is different.

Because it is.

Because I say so.

Whether Tony Blackburn is worse or better than "Opportunity Knocks" is a question I do not wish to discuss. That is not the point at issue.

The point at issue is that whereas it is reasonable, and even commendable to listen to the radio during the day, watching television during the day is immoral, degrading and disgusting.

Because it is.

Because. . . .

Son, are you going to continue these drivelling questions for much longer? I only ask because I would not be averse to five minutes' relaxation.

Then FIND something to do, for goodness sake! Go out and fly your kite.

I don't see what that's got to do with it. WHY can't you fly your kite in the dark?

Because you can't. I see. That's a pretty pathetic argument isn't it?

You know your trouble, lad, don't you? Goggling at all this television has sapped your initiative. When I was your age we used to be out flying kites all night long.

I'll tell you about it another time. Shut up and sit down, I want to watch my favourite programme.

KEITH WATERHOUSE

The poor boy in this 'conversation' can't get a word in edgeways. But you can turn the tables on the father.

1   Read through this one-sided argument again.

2   Then work your way through from the beginning of the piece once more, but this time write down only the *boy's side* of the argument. You may like to try this out in pairs first, role playing as best you can, one as father, one as son. The 'father' reads each of his comments and the 'son' decides how to reply. A casssette recorder might help. See how well you can make the boy stand up to his bossy dad.

Follow on . . .

Think of some other common family arguments, between parents and children, or brothers and sisters. The argument could be over 'suitable' clothes or shoes, 'proper' table manners or what 'time' is 'bedtime'!

Try to write about these arguments in a variety of ways:

- 1   As the writer has done here, just giving one side of the argument.
- 2   As a short play script or story, with both sides being shown.
- 3   As a poem, where you have to reduce your argument and ideas to the barest essentials. A good example is this poem by Michael Rosen.

I'm the youngest in our house
so it goes like this:

My brother comes in and says:
'Tell him to clear the fluff
out from under his bed.'
Mum says,
'Clear the fluff
out from under your bed'
Father says,
'You heard what your mother said.'
  'What?' I say.
  'The fluff,' he says
'Clear the fluff
out from under your bed.'
  So I say,
  'There's fluff under his bed, too,
you know.'
  So father says,
  'But we're talking about the fluff
under *your* bed.'
'You will clear it up
won't you?' mum says.
  So now my brother — all puffed up —
says,
  'Clear the fluff
out from under your bed,
clear the fluff
out from under your bed.'
Now I'm angry. I am angry.
So I say — what shall I say?
'Shuttup stinks
YOU CAN'T RULE MY LIFE.'

Read this poem carefully

The Huntsman

The story is based on a folk tale heard by the author in Kenya in 1944.

Kagwa hunted the lion,
  Through bush and forest went his spear.
One day he found the skull of a man
  And said to it, 'How did you come here?'
The skull opened its mouth and said
  'Talking brought me here.'

Kagwa hurried home;
  Went to the king's chair and spoke:
'In the forest I found a talking skull.'
  The king was silent. Then he said slowly
'Never since I was born of my mother
  Have I seen or heard of a skull which spoke.'

The king called out his guards:
  'Two of you now go with him
And find this talking skull;
  But if his tale is a lie
And the skull speaks no word,
  This Kagwa himself must die.'

They rode into the forest;
  For days and nights they found nothing
At last they saw the skull; Kagwa
  Said to it 'How did you come here?'
The skull said nothing. Kagwa implored,
  But the skull said nothing.

The guards said 'Kneel down.'
  They killed him with sword and spear.
Then the skull opened its mouth;
  'Huntsman, how did you come here?'
And the dead man answered
  'Talking brought me here.'

Edward Lowbury

As you were reading this poem by Edward Lowbury you may have been reminded of those traditional folk tales where adventurers leave home to seek fame and fortune but on the way are forced to submit to a series of 'tests': if successful, they go on to greater glory but if unsuccessful, a fiendish fate awaits them!

Read through the poem again. You may need to read it several times before its meaning starts to become clear — it might help if you acted it out as a drama exercise in small groups.

Then, when you are ready, re-write the poem as a traditional folk tale. You will need to set the scene carefully and create an atmosphere, then go on to build up a sense of tension and suspense by repeating certain key phrases or happenings.

You could keep the original title or change it to anything you consider more suitable — for example, 'The Hunter and the Skull', 'Ask No Questions', 'The Talking Trap'. The choice is yours!

Follow on. . .

Another way in which the sense of the poem can be explored is through a series of pictures or murals.

- 1 Prepare your own set of pictures to explain the meaning of the poem. Before you begin, think carefully about the type of picture you wish to make — collage, drawing, painting or one which uses a mixture of styles. Also decide on the number of pictures you will need — five or six should be about right. Decide too whether you are going to use words in your pictures or just rely on visuals to express feelings and atmosphere.

- 2 Finally, write a short description (to go alongside your pictures) that explains how you were trying to make sense of the poem through your illustrations.

The finished pieces should make an exciting class display.

- 3 *Or* use 'The Huntsman' as a starting point for a poster poem competition. Each member of the class could be asked to design a poster which reflects the feelings and atmosphere of the poem. The words of the poem should be included within the poster but the illustrations and overall design are the important things to concentrate on. The winning poster would be the one which best reflects the feelings and atmosphere of the poem.

Read through these extracts from Tim's diary.

1 How many of Tim's ten questions can *you* answer? Read through his detailed diary entries once again and, working from the information they contain, see how many questions you can complete. (Question 1, on the 'territorial boundaries', has been completed for you.)

2 When you have finished, you can compare your responses with Tim's by turning to page 107.

Follow on . . .

Try keeping your own diary, say over a weekend, which charts the behaviour of one member of your family. You could even set yourself a number of questions that you would like answered.

Be detailed and precise in your report. Time your observations for every hour. Use diagrams as well as words to complete the picture.

You could present a copy of your finished diary to the person you were observing — but first make sure that you have a clear exit to the back door!

Here are some excerpts from *The Diary of a Blackbird* which was written by a fourth year boy over a period of several weeks during the summer term. It begins with a list of questions that he wanted to find out about, then his observations follow, after which he is able to answer the questions he started with.

Blackbird behaviour   Tim (14–15)

These are the questions I want to answer.

1 Territorial boundaries
    (Make a map positioning territory)
2 The food diet
3 His favourite singing posts
4 Does his song differ from the other blackbirds?
5 Which bird incubates the eggs?
6 Behaviour of the male towards the female
7 Behaviour of male towards other females
8 How does the male defend his territory
9 Are there special feeding times
10 Does the male have any special singing times.

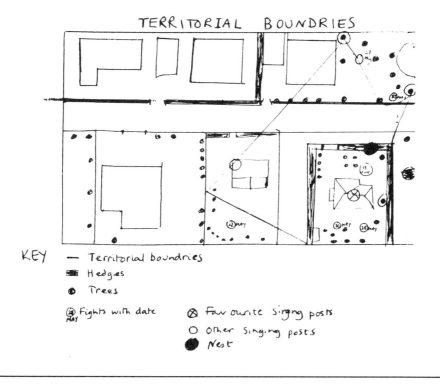

TERRITORIAL BOUNDRIES

KEY   — Territorial boundries
         ▥ Hedges
         ◉ Trees
         ㉕ Fights with date   ⊗ Favourite singing posts
            MAY   ○ Other singing posts
                                    ● Nest

May 20th Monday   12 noon

Male blackbird is singing in the ashtree to the south of the house. After about 5 minutes he flew to the scots pine in the front garden. His song is deepish and musical he sings in bursts of song each around fifteen seconds long. first brood has left the nest.

12.15 pm

Male blackbirds down the road start to sing the blackbird I am studing stops singing.

1.15 pm

Male blackbird feeding in garden on a few berries and worms. I have found a way to distinguish him from other blackbirds. He has a thin white streak down his back and has got a white patch on his left wing. He has also a white patch around his right eye.

May 21st Tuesday   4.15 pm

Male is singing in the ash tree he is facing east. Every time I see him singing he is always facing east or north I think this is because the most arggesive male blackbird is in the north or east.

May 22nd Wednesday   9.00 am

Male blackbird feeding two young ones, while the female is sitting on the nest incubating a second clutch consisting of 3 eggs. it is usually 4.

12.45 pm

Male is on the next doors roof he has just stopped singing. Another Male blackbird has flew up to him. first male flew down to the lawn second Male followed they fluttered into the air, clawing at each other with feet and pecking with their bills, after that they flew off in different directions.

May 25th Saturday   10 am

The male sees another female he flies up to it and he chases her over the cornfield.

11.15 am

Male chase song thrush over cornfield for no apprent reason.

12.15 pm
Male singing on the roof he is facing north. This is his favourite singing post probably because intruders can see him clearly and be warned.

May 27th Monday
Male has been in two fights he has suffered feather loss he's got a bald patch on his back but is still singing strongly the fights were on the east borders of his territory.

May 28th Tuesday   10 am
The male has had another fight in the paddock The other Male blackbird flew off after about 2 minutes.

12.15 pm
Male singing on the roof. The female is incubating the second clutch. This is unusual because the young blackbirds are fed by both parents, then when they leave them, then the female starts to lay another clutch.

May 29th Wednesday   9 am
Male seen with beakful of worms feeds them to the female who is incubating the second cluth of eggs. The male is singing strongly in the mornings around 8 to 9 a.m. and at dinnertime around 11.30 to 1.30 he is also singing late in the evening around 9 p.m.

May 30th Thursday
First brood are still around the male's territory I have only seen 3 when there should be 5. 8.30 pm. Still feeding them. Female is off the nest and has a fight with a male blackbird she did not look as though she had suffered any wounds. It was in the paddock.

May 31st Friday
One of the first brood has been killed by a cat only 4 left. Female is still incubating the second clutch.

20

What comes next? *(Episode 5)*

Fifth Impressions

Here is Episode 5.

P Kevin picked at his supper, but his mother said, 'Do eat up!' and watched him until he finished every morsel. He didn't want food. He wanted Reg.

His mother said, 'And do your homework.' She bustled out of the room. A minute or so later, he heard the TV. She liked that programme, she never missed it! And she wouldn't miss HIM.
He tiptoed to the back door, opened it silently, closed it silently, and was on his way to the big field.

* * *

Q The Captain was within reach. The white parts of the monster glowed pale but clear in the failing light. The Captain muttered 'Climb'. The suit took him up fast.

The Captain had chosen a green spire to climb — a flat-sided spire that would bend when he reached the top of it. The monster was not moving. It was crouched over the remains of the ship. 'Climb. Climb. . . .'

Just as he reached the right place and was about to sway the tip of his spire towards the monster, the monster moved! The Captain made a split-second decision and leaped into nothingness. He stretched his limbs — clutched — and held. Victory!

Gripping one cluster of white or brown or black rods after another, the Captain clambered his way along the monster, making for the brain. It was above the monster's face. He could feel the brain's energy.

He came to the entrance of a tunnel leading into the monster's head and smiled. He clambered into the tunnel, the suit making light work of the journey. Now the brain signals were deafening — even the helmet was overwhelmed. The Captain turned back. He made himself comfortable outside the entrance of the tunnel, anchoring himself securely. He checked some readings and responses. Good. The monster was hearing him.

'You'll enjoy this,' the Captain told the monster. 'You'll like obeying me. You'll like the things we do. You WILL obey me, won't you? Of course you will. You WILL obey me, always. . . .'

* * *

R Kevin found Reg. At first he was glad to find him, but very soon he was puzzled. He kept shaking his head, and he was running. 'He's got a burr in his ear,' thought Kevin. 'Or an insect. An itch.'

Reg was running in regular patterns — a straight line, a pause, a turn to the left, then another straight line, then a pause and a turn to the right. It looked weird in the moonlight. Kevin began to be frightened.

Then Reg suddenly sat down, some ten yards away, and looked straight at Kevin. The dog did not move a muscle. He just stared.

To start you thinking:

● 1 'Gripping one cluster of white or brown or black rods' (section Q). What do you think these 'black rods' are?

● 2 (a) Explain, in your own words, what you think the Captain is doing in section Q.
    (b) A 'tunnel' is mentioned. What do you think that might be?

● 3 Why is Reg behaving so strangely in section R?

● 4 Now make your own notes about this episode. Remember the headings:

* Things you liked
* Things you disliked
* Things that interested you
* Things that surprised you
* Things that confused you
* What might happen next?
* Any other thoughts?

21 *Pictures can talk too*

We often see comic strips similar to this. But how well do the pictures alone tell the story?

1 Working by yourself or in small groups, start by carefully searching each picture frame for story clues. Make notes of what you find. Acting out each frame might help.

2 When you have a feel for the story, begin to write speech for each bubble using your own choice of words.

3 When you have finished, compare your version with those from other groups and with the original which you will find on page 108. But there are not really any right or wrong answers here. What is important is interesting and lively speech that fits in with the illustrations. Choose the best version of all.

Follow on . . .

● 1 Look back at 'Words into pictures' (pages 38–46) and 'How to make comics' (pages 44–46).

● 2 You are the cartoonist responsible for next week's 'Creepy Crawler' story. What can you come up with? To make your task a little easier, use the same setting and characters and just change the story line.

You will need to work through several possibilities in rough before you decide on your final version.

Making sense of 'Cricket in the road

Read this story through a couple of times, by yourself or in small groups.

1 Carefully consider these four statements:
   * This story is mainly about children playing in the rain.
   * This story is mainly about what it feels like to be upset and annoyed.
   * This story is mainly about a boy who is frightened by violent weather.
   * This story is mainly about the pleasure of making up after a quarrel.

   (a) Which of these statements do you agree with most?
   (b) Write down all your reasons for your choice.

2 Look again at lines 4–10, a description of Mayaro (a place on the island of Trinidad) in the rainy season. Pay special attention to the way the writer describes the rainclouds, the winds and the sea.
   (a) Make a list of the descriptive words the writer has chosen — low, grey, scowling and so on.
   (b) Why do you think the writer has chosen these particular words?

3 The very last line of the story reads: 'And I cried as though it were raining and I was afraid.' Why do you think the boy cried?

Follow on . . .

Think back to a moment when you have felt real anger or temper. Take your time, sift through your thoughts and memories until one incident emerges clearly. Then try to describe it in two very different ways:

● 1 As *you* felt and experienced it.

● 2 As somone watching you (a parent, friend or passer-by), might have seen and understood it.

Cricket in the road

In the rainy season we got few chances to play cricket in the road. For whenever we were at the game, the rains came down, chasing us into the yard again.

That was the way it was in Mayaro in the rainy season. The skies were always overcast, and over the sea the rainclouds hung low and grey and scowling, and the winds blew in and whipped angrily through the palms. And when the winds were strongest and raging, the low-hanging clouds would become dense and black, and the sea would roar, and the torrents of rain would come sweeping upon us.

We had just run in from the rain. Amy and Vern from next door were laughing. Amy was in our yard, giggling and pretending to drink the falling rain, with her face all wet and her clothes drenched, and Vern, who was sheltering under the eaves, excitedly jumped out to join her. 'Rain, rain, go to Spain,' they shouted. And soon their mother, who must have heard the noise, appeared from next door, and Vern and Amy vanished through the hedge.

I stood there, depressed about the rain, and then I put Vern's bat and ball underneath the house, and went indoors. 'Fools!' I said to myself. I had been batting when the rains came down. It was only when *I* was batting that the rains came down! I wiped my feet so I wouldn't soil the sheets, and climbed up on the bed. I was sitting, sad, and wishing that the rain would really go away when my heart seemed to jump out of me. A deafening peal of thunder struck across the sky.

Quickly I closed the window. The rain hammered awfully on the roof-top and I kept tense for the thunder which I knew would break again and for the unearthly flashes of lightning.

Secretly I was afraid of the violent weather. I was afraid of the rain, and of the thunder and the lightning that came with them, and of the sea beating against the headlands, and of the storm-winds, and of everything being so strange when the rains were gone. I started again at another flash of lightning and before I had recovered from this, yet another terrifying peal of thunder hit the air. I screamed. Thunder struck again and I dashed under the bed.

'Selo! Selo! First bat!' Vern shouted from the road. The rains had ceased and the sun had come out, but I was not quite recovered yet. I brought myself reluctantly to look out from the front door, and there was Vern, grinning and impatient and beckoning to me.

'First bat,' he said. And as if noting my indifference he looked towards Amy who was just coming out to play. 'Who second bat?' he said.

'Me!' I said.

'Me!' shouted Amy almost at the same time.

'Amy second bat,' Vern said.

'No, I said "Me" first,' I protested.

Vern grew impatient while Amy and I argued. Then an idea seemed to strike him. He took out a penny from his pocket. 'Toss for it,' he said. 'What you want?'

'Heads,' I called.

'Tail,' cried Amy, 'Tail bound to come!'

The coin went up in the air, fell down and overturned, showing tail.

'I'm *not* playing!' I cried, stung. And as that did not seem to disturb enough, I ran towards where I had put Vern's bat and ball and disappeared with them behind our house. Then I flung them with all my strength into the bushes.

When I came back to the front of the house, Vern was standing there dumbfounded. 'Selo, where's the bat and ball?' he said.

I was fuming. 'I don't know about *any* bat and ball!'

'Tell on him,' Amy cried. 'He throw them away.'

Vern's mouth twisted into a forced smile. 'What's an old bat and ball,' he said.

But as he walked out of the yard I saw tears glinting from the corners of his eyes.

For the rest of that rainy season we never played cricket in the road again. Sometimes the rains ceased and the sun came out brightly, and I heard the voices of Amy and Vern on the other side of the fence. At such times I would go out into the road and whistle to myself, hoping they would hear me and come out, but they never did, and I knew they were still very angry and would never forgive me.

And so the rainy season went on. And it was as fearful as ever with the thunder and lightning and waves roaring in the bay, and the strong winds. But the people who talked of all this said that was the way Mayaro was, and they laughed about it. And sometimes when through the rain and even thunder I heard Vern's voice on the other side of the fence, shouting 'Rain, rain, go to Spain,' it puzzled me how it could be so. For often I had made up my mind I would be brave, but when the thunder cracked I always dashed under the bed. It was the beginning of the new year when I saw Vern and Amy again. The rainy season was, happily, long past, and the day was hot and bright and as I walked towards home I saw that I was walking towards Vern and Amy just about to start cricket in the road. My heart thumped violently. They looked strange and new as if they had gone away, far, and did not want to come back any more. They did not notice me until I came up quite near, and then I saw Amy start, her face all lit up.

'Vern—' she cried, 'Vern look—look Selo!'

Embarrassed, I looked at the ground and at the trees, and at the orange sky, and I was so happy I did not know what to say. Vern stared at me, a strange grin on his face. He was ripping the cellophane paper off a brand new bat.

'Selo, here—*you* first bat,' he said gleefully.

And I cried as though it were raining and I was afraid.

MICHAEL ANTHONY

23 | *Scrambled poem*

Read quickly through these two versions of the poem 'Nightmare'.

Somewhere amongst these two scrambled versions, a perfectly decent poem is trying to get out. Can you help it on its way?

1 Working by yourself or in small groups, read through both versions several times. Then work through once more, carefully deciding which line sounds right or makes the best sense, and write it down. Choose each complete line from one version or the other. In this way you will gradually build up your preferred version of the poem.

2 As you, or your group, work through the poems, ask yourself why you prefer one line to the other. Explain your choice, as clearly as you can, on a separate page.

3 When you have finished, compare your selection of lines with those of your friends in other groups.

4 Now look at the original poem which you will find on page 109. Which version do you like best of all? Try to give reasons for your answer.

Follow on . . .

● 1 Most of us have, or have heard about, superstitions and rituals connected with the dark, going to bed, or strange noises in the night. Write about some of your superstitions, either as a poem or a short story.

● 2 (a) Choose a short poem from any book and write your own 'scrambled' version of it. Each line will need to be changed, but not too drastically or else it will be obvious which line is yours and which is the original.

(b) Now shuffle the lines together to get *two* versions, each of which contains some original and some slightly altered lines.

(c) Finally, present the two versions to a friend and see if he or she can detect the original lines from the altered ones. It is not as easy as it seems!

NIGHTMARE

I try not to say his name at all
and refuse to tell anybody
I always close all the drawers
and look behind the door before I get into bed
I cross my toes and count to eight
and turn the pillow over three times
Still he comes sometimes
very quickly
like a shot
glaring at me with his eyes,
scratching me with his nails
and putting on his big sneer —
Mr Scratch

Oh-oh, now I said his name!
Mum, I can't sleep!

NIGHTMARE

I never say his name aloud
and don't tell anybody
I always remember to close all the drawers
and look behind the door before I go to bed
I cross my legs and count to ten
and turn the pillow over many times
Then he comes
one two three
just like that
looking at me with his eyes,
grating with his nails
and sneering his big sneer —
the Scratch Man

Whoops, now his name has slipped out!
I won't be able to sleep now!

What comes next? *(Episode 6)*

Sixth Impressions

Here is Episode 6.

S The Captain halted the monster — the up-and-down motion of the monster's running disturbed his thought — and thought very carefully.

'The monster is a servant creature,' he decided. 'And the upright monster, the one that just arrived, is a superior creature because he makes audio signals and expects them to be obeyed. How do I know that? Because when the upright monster made his signals, my monster was uneasy. He tried to disobey me.' The Captain smiled a little at the thought.

'But does it matter which monster is the master?' he thought. Probably not. They are both much the same size. If they fought, who knows which would win?

'Not that THAT matters much either,' thought the Captain. 'Because I am the controlling brain. So I could appoint either as the master species of the planet. Nevertheless. . . .'

*   *   *

T Kevin shouted 'Reg! Come here when I call you!' But Reg just sat there in the moonlight, staring straight at him, motionless.

Reg said — this time almost pleading — 'Come on, boy. Good boy. Come on Reg. Please.'

But the dog just stared and his eyes looked strange in the moonlight.

*   *   *

U 'Nevertheless,' thought the Captain, 'It might be as well to find out which is master. Besides, one or the other of them might have powerful weapons I should know about. I'll try it.'

He spoke to the dog's brain.

'Kill,' said the Captain. 'Kill that other creature there.'

To get you started:

- 1 Who, or what, is the 'upright monster' that has 'just arrived' (section S)?

- 2 Why should it matter to the Captain which is the 'superior creature'?

- 3 How does section S leave you wanting to read on?

- 4 There is only one episode left. How would you end this story?

- 5 Now make your own notes about this episode. Remember the headings:

* Things you liked
* Things you disliked
* Things that interested you
* Things that surprised you
* Things that confused you
* What might happen next?
* Any other thoughts?

Look carefully at the photograph below.

1 Write down the six most important things you can see in this photo.

2 Where might you find a photo like this? In a magazine? A newspaper? A family album? An advertisement? Give as many reasons as you can for your choice.

From rough to best

On the next page we have the first draft of a poem (A), by Michael Rosen, and the final, published version (B). Read them both through carefully twice. Then answer the following questions in small groups or by yourself.

1   Make a list of all the lines the writer cut out from his first attempt (A).

2   Make a list of all the completely new lines added to (B).

3   Most of the early lines in (A) were later left out of (B). Why do you think the writer rejected these lines?

4   Would you have kept any of these rejected lines? If yes, which ones and why? If no, why not?

5   (a) Now look at your list of new lines added to (B). Did you include the title? What do you think of it?
    (b) In what ways is it better or different from 'My father's father'?

6   Michael Rosen obviously liked the line 'a hulky bulky thick check jacket', as it is in both versions. Quickly write down or draw what you see in your 'mind's eye' when you say those six words.

7   'a few old papers, a few old photos' – why might these things have suddenly arrived, along with the jacket, 'One day in spring'?

8   '. . . the man
    I would have called "Grandad".
    The Man Who Stayed Behind.'
    Read the *final six lines* of the finished poem (B) again.
    What do you think were the real reasons for the writer liking the jacket so much?

Follow on . . .

Think of an object that reminds you of something or someone special. Try to remember the details of where you found it or when you were given it.

● 1   Organize your memories into a short piece of writing, describing how this object became so special for you.

● 2   Then try to compress your ideas and feelings even more, by writing a poem. Remember that a second draft will often make things much clearer.

(First Attempt)

My father's father

my father came to England
my father's sister came to England
one of my father's brothers came to
  England
one of my father's brothers stayed

my father's mother came to England
but my father's father stayed behind,
along with the other brother.
my father, my father's sister, and one of
  the brothers
They waited and they waited —
for them to cross the sea and come
but my father's father
wrote to say he was too busy to come
he said there was too much to do
so my dad had no dad here
and I never saw that grandad
though one day in spring
some things arrived instead
A few papers, a few photos
and the most beautiful — o yes —
a hulky bulky thick check jacket
that I want to wear
very very very very very much.

(Finished Poem)

NEWCOMERS

My father came to England
from another country
My father's mother came to England
from another country
but my father's father
stayed behind.

So my dad had no dad here
and I never saw him at all.

One day in spring
some things arrived:
a few old papers,
a few old photos
and – oh yes –
a hulky bulky thick checked jacket
that belonged to the man
I would have called 'Grandad'.
The Man Who Stayed Behind.

But I kept that jacket
and I wore it
and I wore it
and I wore it
till it wore right through
at the back.

84

Look back at the photograph on page 82. Now look at the photograph on the next page. As you can see, a caption has now been added to the original photo.

1 Does this make any difference to what you now see in the photo?

2 Where might you see a photo with a caption like this?

3 Have you changed your mind about where you might see this photo, since answering question 2 on page 82? Give reasons for your answer.

He never hears a word his mother says. And he never will.

Madabout

Where do rabbits who are mad about motor racing go?

RACING

GUEST STAR

KEITH CHEGWIN, star of television and radio shows, used to have a kart but he never actually raced in it. He would put it in the boot of his car and dash off to a nearby airfield where he could drive around to his heart's content. Unfortunately, one day he got carried away and wandered on to the runway — preventing any planes from landing!

DID YOU KNOW . . .
. . . that the first motor race took place in France in 1894? It was won by Count de Dion who drove a de Dion steam vehicle from Paris to Rouen at a speed of 11.6mph!

Hurtling along at 60 mph only 15mm (½in) above the ground may not be everyone's idea of fun, but for **karting** enthusiasts it's the only way to travel.

The Northumbria Karting Club at Felton, near Morpeth, occupies an old World War Two bomber base where a twisting tarmac track is laid out on the concrete airstrip. Race meetings are held there regularly and last for most of the day, starting at 9.30am with a practice session and ending at around 4.00pm with the final race.

The karts are pushed off from a dummy grid, then they drive round to the start-line which is about three-quarters of the way round the circuit. At the start the drivers line up in predetermined positions in two rows of four karts. Three heats are raced like this and the results of these determine the drivers' starting positions for the final.

The karts are divided into different groups, according to engine and gearbox types. Juniors, who start racing from the age of 11, drive either 100cc Britain karts or 100cc National karts – both are non-gearbox types. You need to have an RAC karting licence to drive, and it's a pretty expensive hobby: a new kart plus driving suit (leathers, boots, helmet, etc) can cost up to £900.

Although the sport looks pretty lethal, karters say that it isn't dangerous – provided you know what you're doing and are well disciplined. Very few accidents occur and it's virtually impossible for a kart to turn over because of its low centre of gravity and wide wheelbase – it clings to the road surface like glue!

DID YOU KNOW . . .
. . . that the world's fastest spider can cover 33 times its own body length per second? If a man could do the same he would be able to sprint at a speed of 135 mph!
A snail going flat out would take eleven days to cover a distance of one mile !

Matthew with lady racing driver Wendy Slattery.

Matthew gets a few tips on racing from behind the wheel of Wendy's car.

WOMAN ON WHEELS

One of the best known forms of racing is **motor racing**, which is usually associated with men. However, 20-year-old Wendy Slattery is hoping to change all that.

She started her racing driving career at the Brands Hatch Racing School in Kent where she learned to drive a Formula Ford, a one-seater racing car. It's quite expensive to learn at the school – it cost Wendy about £600. However, she doesn't think that is the reason why there are so few women racing drivers – rather that women feel that it's a sport for men only.

Which is, of course, rubbish! Wendy's car travels at about 120mph – and she's won several races in it – including ones where she was the only woman taking part. Like all racing drivers, Wendy has had a few crashes, but these don't actually bother her now as she has become used to them. All she thinks about is how much it's going to cost to get the car fixed!

SEASIDE SPEED

From four wheels to two and racing on a rather unusual surface . . . **Sand racing** is a bit like scrambling, only you race on – guess what? – sand!

Redcar Sands, where the Tyne Tees Motor Cycle Sand Racing Club meets, are famous for land speed records, dating back to 1928. Races usually start around four hours before high tide. It's nearly always cold and windy, but they can go ahead in any weather conditions except fog. Riders prepare their bikes on the promenade before the races. Once they are happy with them, the bikes are checked thoroughly by the officials for safety, after which the riders can drive down to the pits and have two practice laps before the race.

Juniors, who can start from the age of six, ride 100 to 125cc bikes, for which they need a licence. Although it's not a cheap sport, it is the least expensive form of motor-bike racing.

87

Making sense of 'Madabout'

This is a magazine centre-spread, linked to the ITV series 'Madabout', hosted by Matthew Kelley.

It covers one particular programme in the series, on 'Racing'.

As you read it, think about where your eye is drawn — what you look at first and where you go next. Then draw a sketch of the spread and draw arrows to show how you read it.

Spend some time in small groups discussing the way the spread is displayed. Then consider these points:

1 (a) Why do you think the article is laid out in this way?
   (b) Why include the joke at the top of the page and the cartoon in the middle right?
   (c) Why include a photograph of Keith Chegwin, with the headline: 'Guest Star'?
   (d) What has been done to prevent the spread being boring?

2 Can you see any similarities with the 'Wildtrack' spread on page 17, where a similar attempt was made to be informative and entertaining? List some of the similarities and differences.

3 In the brief article on 'Karting' most information is given for one particular age group.
   (a) Which age group is this?
   (b) Why do you think this age group was concentrated on?

4 The piece headed 'Woman on Wheels' gives Wendy Slattery's opinion on why there are so few women racing drivers.
   (a) What is her opinion?
   (b) Do you agree with her? Give reasons for your answer.

5 Costs and expense are mentioned in all three articles. Why do you think this is?

Follow on . . .

Use the example of the 'Madabout' display spread to help you design a centre-page piece on a hobby or activity of your own choosing.

Your presentation needs to include useful information and entertaining items that people of your age group would want to read about.

You could also display some interviews, photographs, even jokes and cartoons. Anything, in fact, to make your centre-page lively and interesting.

Picture predictions *(3)*

Look back at the photographs on pages 82 and 85. Now look at the photograph on the next page. The picture is now complete.

1 It states that some types of deafness can be helped by wearing a hearing aid, but problems remain. What is the biggest problem?

2 Briefly describe the three other kinds of deafness mentioned in the poster.

3 What is the main point about deafness that this poster is trying to get across?

4 What are the two things the RNID are asking you to do?

Follow on . . .

• 1 Do you think this is an effective poster? Could you have done any better?

• 2 Design a poster for the RNID aimed at people your own age. You can use any of the information on the original poster, but keep it simple and eyecatching. The main thing is to design a picture and a caption which will start people thinking about some of the problems deaf people have to face.

He never hears
a word his mother says.
And he never will.

If we say he's deaf, you'll probably think, Poor kid, but it might have been a lot worse.

Think again.

If he's totally deaf, he won't hear his own voice, let alone anyone else's. A hearing aid will be useless. Life will be like a silent film, without captions.

If his disability is not so severe and he is able to wear a hearing aid, it could still be like spending every moment of every day listening to a 'phone call on a bad line.

If he learns to lip read, he will have to guess what's being said because so many mouth movements look the same. For example P, B and M as in Pat, Bat and Mat.

If he suffers from one kind of deafness he'll hear only vowels. 'The most desperate of human calamities' will sound like,'E oh e uh a o oo a a a i i'.

If he suffers from another kind of deafness he won't hear quiet sounds, but loud sounds will cause him great pain. Life won't be made any easier by

friends who know 'he's a little deaf' and shout all the time.

Deafness is maybe a lot worse than most of us think.

If you want to do something, give money to the RNID so that we may continue our work. At least give more consideration to the deaf. Even better, give both.

RNID. The Royal National Institute for the Deaf.

Send your donation to: RNID, Room 2L, 105 Gower Street, London WC1E 6AH. Telephone 01-387 8033.

Story into script

Stories are often changed into play scripts for use on stage or with drama groups. They can also be re-worked into 'story boards' or 'shooting scripts' and used as a basis for film or television productions. What follows is part of the opening chapter of *Flat Stanley* by Jeff Brown. As with many stories about changing shape or size, it was originally written for younger children but can be enjoyed by people of any age.

Immediately following the story extract is a version of the same piece written as a play script. Here, everything except the short introductory statement is written as speech, with one person talking aloud to another.

Carefully read both pieces. A really close look will show that several things have been changed moving from story into script.

Breakfast was ready.

'I will go and wake the boys,' Mrs Lambchop said to her husband, George Lambchop. Just then their younger son, Arthur, called from the bedroom he shared with his brother Stanley in their New York home.

'Hey! Come and look! Hey!'

Mr and Mrs Lambchop were both very much in favour of politeness and careful speech. 'Hay is for horses, Arthur, not people,' Mr Lambchop said as they entered the bedroom. 'Try to remember that.'

'Excuse me,' Arthur said. 'But look!'

He pointed to Stanley's bed. Across it lay the enormous bulletin board that Mr Lambchop had given the boys a Christmas ago, so that they could pin up pictures and messages and maps. It had fallen, during the night, on top of Stanley.

But Stanley was not hurt. In fact he would still have been sleeping if he had not been woken by his brother's shout.

'What's going on here?' he called out cheerfully from beneath the enormous board.

Mr and Mrs Lambchop hurried to lift it from the bed.

'Heavens!' said Mrs Lambchop.

'Gosh!' said Arthur. 'Stanley's flat!'

'As a pancake,' said Mr Lambchop. 'Darndest thing I've ever seen.'

'Let's all have breakfast,' Mrs Lambchop said. 'Then Stanley and I will go and see Doctor Dan and hear what he has to say.'

Mrs Lambchop	Breakfast is ready, George. I'll go and wake the boys.
Mr Lambchop	I think I can hear one of them calling. ★
Mrs Lambchop	Yes, it's young Arthur. He's using that word, 'Hey!' again. Listen! ★
Arthur	Hey! Come and look! Hey!
Mrs Lambchop	I wish he wouldn't use that word. It isn't a nice word at all. Stanley never uses words like, 'Hey!'
Mr Lambchop	He's calling louder than ever now. ★ There must be something wrong.
Arthur	Hey! Come and look! Hey!
Mr Lambchop	I think we'd better go up to the boys' bedroom.
Arthur	Hey! Come and look! Hey!
Mrs Lambchop	We're coming, Arthur. And don't keep shouting, 'Hey!' *Hay* is for horses, not people. Try to remember that. You should say, 'Excuse me.'
Arthur	Excuse me! But look!
Mrs Lambchop	Heavens! That enormous notice board we gave the boys last Christmas is lying right across Stanley's bed.
Mr Lambchop	Gosh! It must have fallen down during the night and now it's right on top of Stanley.
Mrs Lambchop	Don't stand there talking, George. Help me to lift it up. ★ Our son is underneath that board and I want him out.
Arthur	Stanley! Stanley! Where are you? I can see him. Come on, Stanley. Come out.
Stanley	What's going on? Why are you all staring at me? Why are you all staring at me like that?
Arthur	Gosh! Look at him!
Mrs Lambchop	Heavens! He's been squashed flat.
Mr Lambchop	Gosh! Stanley's flat. He's as flat as a pancake.

Mrs Lambchop	I've never seen anything like this before in all my life.
Stanley	I may be flat, but I'm quite okay.
Mrs Lambchop	Of course you're not, dear. You're flat and you're hurt.
Stanley	I'm not hurt. I'm just flat. I want my breakfast.
Mr Lambchop	The boy wants his breakfast, so he's not too bad. Boys who want their breakfast aren't too bad.
Arthur	He's not too bad if he wants his breakfast.
Mrs Lambchop	All right. But the minute we've had our breakfast, we'll go round and see Dr Dan and hear what he has to say.

1 Make a list of all the words and phrases that have been added to the play script (i.e., that were not in the original story version).

2 Write down all the changes that have occurred between the two versions such as one person saying something in the story but a different person saying it in the play.

3 After discussing these lists in small groups, write down as many reasons as you can to explain why these changes and additions have occurred. For instance, why does 'bulletin board' in the story become 'notice board' in the play script? And why does Stanley say so much more in the play version?

What follows is a further scene from the story version. Read it through a couple of times, then, by yourself or in small groups, attempt your own play script based on this scene. You can, of course, change things around and add new speech of your own, if you think it makes your script version better.

Being flat could also be helpful, Stanley found.

He was taking a walk with Mrs Lambchop one afternoon when her favourite ring fell from her finger. The ring rolled across the pavement and down between the bars of a grating that covered a dark, deep shaft. Mrs Lambchop began to cry.

'I have an idea,' Stanley said.

He took the laces out of his shoes and an extra pair out of his pocket and tied them all together to make one long lace. Then he tied the end of that to the back of his belt and gave the other end to his mother.

'Lower me,' he said, 'and I will look for the ring.'

'Thank you, Stanley,' Mrs Lambchop said. She lowered him between the bars and moved him carefully up and down and from side to side, so that he could search the whole floor of the shaft.

Two policemen came by and stared at Mrs Lambchop as she stood holding the long lace that ran down through the grating. She pretended not to notice them.

'What's the matter, lady?' the first policeman asked. 'Is your yo-yo stuck?'

'I am not playing with a yo-yo!' Mrs Lambchop said sharply. 'My son is at the other end of this lace, if you must know.'

'Humour her, Harry,' said the second policeman. 'The poor soul's dotty as can be!'

Just then, down in the shaft, Stanley cried out, 'Hooray!'

Mrs Lambchop pulled him up and saw that he had the ring.

'Good for you, Stanley,' she said. Then she turned angrily to the policemen.

'Dotty, indeed!' she said. 'Shame!'

The policemen apologized. 'We didn't get it, lady,' they said. 'We have been hasty. We see that now.'

'People should think twice before making rude remarks,' said Mrs Lambchop. 'And then not make them at all.'

The policemen realized that was a good rule and said they would try to remember it.

When you have finished, you can compare your script with those of other groups, and with the published version, which you will find on page 110. The differences could be interesting.

Follow on . . .

By now you should be fairly familiar with 'Flat Stanley' and his 'problem'.

- 1 Write some 'Further Adventures of Flat Stanley' either as a story or as a play script, where Stanley uses his flatness to get out of trouble or to achieve something he would normally be unable to do. List a few ideas in rough to start you thinking. You could also add some simple illustrations to give extra interest to your writing.

- 2 How could you end a story about 'Flat Stanley'? Presumably, he ends up back in his normal shape — but how might it happen? Write down some ideas. Then choose the idea you like best and develop it either in story or play form.

What comes next? (Episode 7)

Seventh impressions – final comment

Here is Episode 7.

V The dog attacked. 'Reg!' yelled Kevin. 'Don't, Reg!'

Reg over-ran him and turned and charged again, snarling like a hound of hell. And then the dog had hurtled the boy to the ground and was standing over him, jaws open, teeth bared.

'Reg!' It was a scream of terror.

The dog paused. The big voice in his head said 'KILL!' but the old, loved, familiar voice was calling too, asking for help.

The dog paused; the boy struck out blindly with his fist. He hit the dog's ear. Something small fell to the ground, unseen. The little thing was mortally wounded. It writhed.

Reg said 'Woof!' in a vague way and looked at Kevin. The dog licked the boy's face, wagged his tail and sheepishly got off Kevin's chest. He sat down and scratched his ear with a hind paw. But the itching had gone.

The little, unseen thing writhed for the last time; and, hidden in the grass, the Captain died.

The boy and the dog rollicked off together across the moonlit field. Sometimes the boy chased the dog: sometimes the dog chased the boy. When they got home, they were both scolded by Kevin's mother.

         *   *   *

W By the edge of the trees, the dew was heavy on the spaceship. Soon it would rust and become as brown as the earth. But now it was still shiny and glinting in the tall weeds. In the moonlight, you wouldn't have noticed where its body was crushed and dented. It looked like a super-perfect model. Little, but marvellously made.

---

1   Well? Did the story work out just as you predicted?

2   Did this particular ending satisfy you?

3   Again, think through those headings:

* Things you liked
* Things you disliked
* Things that interested you
* Things that surprised you
* Things that confused you

4   (a) What sort of reader do you think would enjoy a story like this?
    (b) What sort of reader might not enjoy a story like this?

5   What changes or improvements would you like to make to the story?

Follow on . . .

Try writing your own 'twin-track' story, where the action keeps cross-cutting from one story thread to another.

A lot of planning is needed before you start, however, as the threads should come together at some point, but not necessarily at the end.

Twin-track or cross-cutting methods can be particularly good at creating an atmosphere of surprise, excitement or suspense and this might affect the kind of story you attempt to write. Good luck!

32 | *Asking your own questions*

Read through this story carefully, perhaps in small groups.

Now you, or your group, can have the job of asking some of your own questions on this one.

Start by going through the story again, but make a list of all the things you find puzzling, interesting or important. Then try to shape these thoughts into five or six most helpful questions that you would like to know the answer to and which would help you make more sense of the story.

For example, your questions might look like this.

1 Why did William's mother go to the clinic?

2 How old is William? What evidence is there?

3 What three words of your own would best describe the behaviour of (a) William and (b) his Granny?

4 Why does William behave in the way he does?

5 Can William read? How do we know?

6 Has Granny changed by the end of the story? In what ways?

Which questions would you like to ask? You may use these ideas to get you started, but your own questions are likely to be most helpful for you.

Follow on . . .

William's own version of 'The Three Little Pigs' formed an important part of the story you have just read.

Try writing your own version of a well-known or traditional story.

- You could re-write 'Red Riding Hood', but this time with the wolf as the hero!

- An intelligent and brave Princess could rescue a puny Prince from captivity.

- Cinderella's older sisters could be the ones having a hard time, all because of that goody-goody youngster!

98

6 William's Version

William and Granny were left to entertain each other for an hour while William's mother went to the clinic.

'Sing to me,' said William.

'Granny's too old to sing,' said Granny.

'I'll sing to you, then,' said William. William only knew one song. He had forgotten the words and the tune, but he sang it several times, anyway.

'Shall we do something else now?' said Granny.

'Tell me a story,' said William. 'Tell me about the wolf.'

'Red Riding Hood?'

'No, not *that* wolf, the other wolf.'

'Peter and the wolf?' said Granny.

'Mummy's going to have a baby,' said William.

'I know,' said Granny.

William looked suspicious.

'How do you know?'

'Well . . . she told me. And it shows, doesn't it?'

'The lady down the road had a baby. It looks like a pig,' said William. He counted on his fingers. 'Three babies looks like three pigs.'

'Ah,' said Granny. 'Once upon a time there were three little pigs. Their names were – '

'They didn't have names,' said William.

'Yes they did. The first pig was called – '

'Pigs don't have names.'

'Some do. These pigs had names.'

'No they didn't.' William slid off Granny's lap and went to open the corner cupboard by the fireplace. Old magazines cascaded out as old magazines do when they have been flung into a cupboard and the door slammed shut. He rooted among them until he found a little book covered with brown paper, climbed into the cupboard, opened the book, closed it and climbed out again. 'They didn't have names,' he said.

'I didn't know you could read,' said Granny, properly impressed.

'C – A – T, wheelbarrow,' said William.

'Is that the book Mummy reads to you out of?'

'It's my book,' said William.

'But it's the one Mummy reads?'

'If she says please,' said William.

'Well, that's Mummy's story, then. My pigs have names.'

'They're the wrong pigs.' William was not open to negotiation. 'I don't want them in this story.'

'Can't we have different pigs this time?'

'No. They won't know what to do.'

'Once upon a time,' said Granny, 'there were three little pigs who lived with their mother.'

'Their mother was dead,' said William.

'Oh, I'm sure she wasn't,' said Granny.

'She was dead. You make bacon out of dead pigs. She got eaten for breakfast and they threw the rind out for the birds.'

'So the three little pigs had to find homes for themselves.'

'No.' William consulted his book. 'They had to build little houses.'

'I'm just coming to that.'

'You said they had to *find* homes. They didn't *find* them.'

'The first little pig walked along for a bit until he met a man with a load of hay.'

'It was a lady.'

'A lady with a load of hay?'

'N O ! It was a lady-pig. You said *he*.'

'I thought all the pigs were little boy-pigs,' said Granny.

'It says lady-pig here,' said William. 'It says the lady-pig went for a walk and met a man with a load of hay.'

'So the lady-pig,' said Granny, 'said to the man,

"May I have some of that hay to build a house?" and the man said, "Yes." Is that right?'

'Yes,' said William. 'You know that baby?'

'What baby?'

'The one Mummy's going to have. Will that baby have shoes on when it comes out?'

'I don't think so,' said Granny.

'It will have cold feet,' said William.

'Oh no,' said Granny. 'Mummy will wrap it up in a soft shawl, all snug.'

'I don't *mind* if it has cold feet,' William explained. 'Go on about the lady-pig.'

'So the little lady-pig took the hay and built a little house. Soon the wolf came along and the wolf said – '

'You didn't tell where the wolf lived.'

'I don't know where the wolf lived.'

'15 Tennyson Avenue, next to the bomb-site,' said William.

'I bet it doesn't say that in the book,' said Granny, with spirit.

'Yes it does.'

'Let me see, then.'

William folded himself up with his back to Granny, and pushed the book up under his pullover.

'*I* don't think it says that in the book,' said Granny.

'It's in ever so small words,' said William.

'So the wolf said, "Little pig, little pig, let me come in," and the little pig answered, "No". So the wolf said, "Then I'll huff and I'll puff and I'll blow your house down," and he huffed and he puffed and he blew the house down, and the little pig ran away.'

'He ate the little pig,' said William.

'No, no,' said Granny. 'The little pig ran away.'

'He ate the little pig. He ate her in a sandwich.'

'All right, he ate the little pig in a sandwich. So the second little pig – '

'You didn't tell about the tricycle.'

'What about the tricycle?'

'The wolf got on his tricycle and went to the bread

shop to buy some bread. To make the sandwich,' William explained, patiently.

'Oh well, the wolf got on his tricycle and went to the bread shop to buy some bread. And he went to the grocer's to buy some butter.' This innovation did not go down well.

'He already had some butter in the cupboard,' said William.

'So then the second little pig went for a walk and met a man with a load of wood, and the little pig said to the man, "May I have some of that wood to build a house?" and the man said, "Yes." '

'He didn't say please.'

' "Please may I have some of that wood to build a house?" '

'It was sticks.'

'Sticks *are* wood.'

William took out his book and turned the pages. 'That's right,' he said.

'Why don't you tell the story?' said Granny.

'I can't remember it,' said William.

'You could read it out of your book.'

'I've lost it,' said William, clutching his pullover. 'Look, do you know who this is?' He pulled a green angora scarf from under the sofa.

'No, who is it?' said Granny, glad of the diversion.

'This is Doctor Snake.' He made the scarf wriggle across the carpet.

'Why is he a doctor?'

'Because he is all furry,' said William. He wrapped the doctor round his neck and sat sucking the loose end. 'Go on about the wolf.'

'So the little pig built a house of sticks and along came the wolf – on his tricycle?'

'He came by bus. He didn't have any money for a ticket so he ate up the conductor.'

'That wasn't very nice of him,' said Granny.

'No,' said William. 'It wasn't *very* nice.'

'And the wolf said, "Little pig, little pig, let me come

in," and the little pig said, "No," and the wolf said, "Then I'll huff and I'll puff and I'll blow your house down," so he huffed and he puffed and he blew the house down. And then what did he do?' Granny asked, cautiously.

William was silent.

'Did he eat the second little pig?'

'Yes.'

'How did he eat this little pig?' said Granny, prepared for more pig sandwiches or possibly pig on toast.

'With his mouth,' said William.

'Now the third little pig went for a walk and met a man with a load of bricks. And the little pig said, "*Please* may I have some of those bricks to build a house?" and the man said, "Yes." So the little pig took the bricks and built a house.'

'He built it on the bomb-site.'

'Next door to the wolf?' said Granny. 'That was very silly of him.'

'There wasn't anywhere else,' said William. 'All the roads were full up.'

'The wolf didn't have to come by bus or tricycle this time, then, did he?' said Granny, grown cunning.

'Yes.' William took out the book and peered in, secretively. 'He was playing in the cemetery. He had to get another bus.'

'And did he eat the conductor this time?'

'No. A nice man gave him some money, so he bought a ticket.'

'I'm glad to hear it,' said Granny.

'He ate the nice man,' said William.

'So the wolf got off the bus and went up to the little pig's house, and he said, "Little pig, little pig, let me come in," and the little pig said, "No," and then the wolf said, "I'll huff and I'll puff and I'll blow your house down," and he huffed and he puffed and he huffed and he puffed but he couldn't blow the house down because it was made of bricks.'

'He couldn't blow it down,' said William, 'because it was stuck to the ground.'

'Well, anyway, the wolf got very cross then, and he climbed on the roof and shouted down the chimney, "I'm coming to get you!" but the little pig just laughed and put a big saucepan of water on the fire.'

'He put it on the gas stove.'

'He put it on the *fire*,' said Granny, speaking very rapidly, 'and the wolf fell down the chimney and into the pan of water and was boiled and the little pig ate him for supper.'

William threw himself full length on the carpet and screamed.

'He didn't! He didn't! *He didn't*! He didn't eat the wolf.'

Granny picked him up, all stiff and kicking, and sat him on her lap.

'Did I get it wrong again, love? Don't cry. Tell me what really happened.'

William wept, and wiped his nose on Doctor Snake.

'The little pig put the saucepan on the gas stove and the wolf got down the chimney and put the little pig in the saucepan and boiled him. He had him for tea, with chips,' said William.

'Oh,' said Granny. 'I've got it all wrong, haven't I? Can I see the book, then I shall know, next time.'

William took the book from under his pullover. Granny opened it and read, *First Aid for Beginners: a Practical Handbook.*

'I see,' said Granny. 'I don't think I can read this. I left my glasses at home. You tell Gran how it ends.'

William turned to the last page which showed a prostrate man with his leg in a splint; *compound fracture of the femur.*

'Then the wolf washed up and got on his tricycle and went to see his Granny, and his Granny opened the door and said, "Hello, William."'

'I thought it was the wolf.'

'It was. It was the wolf. His name was William Wolf,' said William.

'What a nice story,' said Granny. 'You tell it much better than I do.'

'I can see up your nose,' said William. 'It's all whiskery.'

Answers

Chapter 2 (page 12)

Chapter 6 (page 28)

The School Caretaker

In the corner of the playground
Down dark and slimy stairs,
Lived a monster with a big nose
Full of curly hairs.

He had a bunch of keyrings
Carved out of little boys,
He confiscated comics
And all our favourite toys.

He wore a greasy uniform,
Looked like an undertaker,
More scary than a horror film,
He was the school caretaker.

I left the school some years ago;
Saw him again the other day.
He looked rather sad and old
Shuffling on his way.

It's funny when you grow up
How grown-ups start growing down,
And the snarls upon their faces
Are no more than a frown.

In the corner of the playground
Down dark and slimy stairs,
Sits a lonely little man
With a nose full of curly hairs.

Chapter 19 (page 66)

The diary continues throughout June. Then comes a heading:
Answers to my questions

  1 my answer to question one is on the territorial map.

  2 *Their food diet*

Their food consists of mainly fruit grown in gardens and also wild fruit and they had the buds off apple and pear trees. they fed the young on mainly insects, earthworms etc.

  3 *The males singing post*
When he is singing his favourite singing post is on our roof always facing north or east but never west or south. My answer is that the two most aggressive males are to the north and east whereas the less aggressive are to the south and west.

  4 *Song difference from other males*
It is hard to tell really because each song is a little different from the other songs. His song is deep and he sings in shorter bursts of song than the other surrounding male birds.

5 *Which bird incubates the eggs?*
   The female does all the incubating she gets off the nest every early morning and at dusk to feed and exercise her wings.

6 *Behaviour of male towards the female*
   The males atitued towards the female is gentle and friendly and I didn't see any aggression against each other.

7 *Behaviour of male towards other females*
   The aggression is mostly turned to the males but the male blackbird did show aggressive behaviour towards females sometimes.

8 *How does the male defend his territory?*
   He defends it mainly by song but he has had fights over it mainly when the female was incubating the eggs.

9 *Are there special feeding times?*
   No, there isn't they feed when is nessersary and only take the adequate amount.

10 *Does the male have any special singing times?*
   Yes, he is singing mainly early in the morning singing around midday and then again in the evening. Each time he sings no more than 45 minutes.

Chapter 21 (page 72)

Chapter 23 (page 78)

Nightmare

I never say his name aloud
and don't tell anybody
I always close all the drawers
and look behind the door before I go to bed
I cross my toes and count to eight
and turn the pillow over three times
Still he comes sometimes
one two three
like a shot
glaring at me with his eyes,
grating with his nails
and sneering his big sneer—
the Scratch Man

Oh-oh, now I said his name!
Mum, I can't sleep!

Chapter 30 (page 91)

Mrs Lambchop	Stay on the pavement, boys. Owwwww! I've dropped my ring. It's rolling across the pavement towards that grating. ★ Quick! Get it!
Stanley	Arthur! Arthur! Get it quickly.
Arthur	I can't. It's gone.
Mrs Lambchop	Oh Stanley! Oh Arthur! It's my favourite ring and now it's dropped between the bars of the grating. It must be down at the bottom of the shaft.
Stanley	Don't cry! I have an idea. Look! I've got some laces in my pocket. I'll tie them together. Now I'll take the laces out of my shoes and make one very long string.
Mrs Lambchop	What are you going to do, Stanley?
Stanley	I'm going to tie one end of the long lace I've made to the back of my belt. You hold the other end. Now, slide me down.
Mrs Lambchop	Do you mean I've got to lower you down between the bars?
Stanley	Yes, that's it. I'm so flat, you can slide me down between the bars so that I can look for the ring. ★
Policeman	Hullo, hullo! What's going on here? What's the matter, lady? Is your yo-yo stuck?
Mrs Lambchop	I'm not holding a yo-yo. I'm holding my son, Stanley.
Policeman	I've never seen a lady holding a shoe lace over a grating before. This son of yours must be a very funny shape.
Mrs Lambchop	Shame on you. My son is searching for my ring. Not every mother has a flat son to send looking for lost rings.
Policeman	I'd better be careful what I say to this poor soul. Are you sure you feel all right, lady?
Mrs Lambchop	Of course I'm all right. It's my son who's not all right. He's down there in the dark.
Policeman	The poor soul's as dotty as can be!
Stanley	Hooray! I've got it! Pull me up! ★

110

Arthur	Good for you, Stanley.
Stanley	Whoops! Here I am! And here's the ring.
Policeman	I didn't get it lady. I'm sorry.
Mrs Lambchop	I know you didn't get it. My son's the one who went down and got it.
Policeman	I mean, I didn't understand.
Mrs Lambchop	Dotty, indeed! You called me dotty. Shame!
Policeman	I was too hasty. I see that now, and I can see that you have a very flat son.
Mrs Lambchop	People should think twice before they make rude remarks, and then not make them at all.
Policeman	That's a very good rule, lady. I'll make a note of that and remember it.

Hutchinson Education
An imprint of Century Hutchinson Ltd
62–65 Chandos Place, London WC2N 4NW

Century Hutchinson Publishing Group
(Australia) Pty Ltd
16–22 Church Street, Hawthorn, Melbourne,
Victoria 3122

Century Hutchinson Group (NZ) Ltd
32–34 View Road, PO Box 40–086, Glenfield,
Auckland 10

Century Hutchinson (SA) (Pty) Ltd
PO Box 337, Bergvlei 2012, South Africa.

First published 1986

© Mike Hamlin 1986

Set in Linotron Sabon
by Input Typesetting Ltd, London
Printed and bound in Great Britain by Scotprint

British Library Cataloguing in Publication Data
Hamlin, Mike
   Steps in understanding.
   Bk. 1
   1. English language——Examinations,
questions, etc.
   I. Title
   428.2   PE1112

ISBN 0 09 167971 0

Acknowledgements

The Publishers' thanks are due to the following for permission to reproduce copyright material:

Chapter 1: William Collins Sons & Co. Ltd for 'The Best of Enemies' from *Challenge in the Dark* by Robert Leeson; *Chapter 2*: Cambridge University Press for extract from *The Long Distance Poet* by Jan Mark, illustrated by Steve Smallman, published by Cambridge Educational; *Chapter 5*: The author for 'The ant-lion' by Judith Wright; *Chapter 7*: Jonathan Cape Ltd for 'Unscratchable Itch' by Shel Silverstein, from *A Light in the Attic* by Shel Silverstein, illustrated by the author: *Chapter 9*: J M Dent & Sons Ltd for 'Trouble in the Supermarket' from *Nonstop Nonsense* by Margaret Mahy; *Chapter 10*: The author for 'Guy Fawkes' by Barry Heath; *Chapter 11*: Victor Gollancz Ltd for 'My Very Strange Teeth' from *The Julian Stories* by Ann Cameron; James Morrow for comic strip, 'Professor Mindboggle tells how to make comics'; *Chapter 14*: The Bodley Head for 'Self-portrait of a computer nut' from *The Computer Nut* by Betsy Byars, illustration by Guy Byars; *Chapter 15*: William Heinemann Ltd for 'News' and illustration from *Funny Folk* by Aidan Chambers; *Chapter 17*: David Higham Associates Ltd for 'Watch with Father' from *Mondays, Thursdays* by Keith Waterhouse, published by Michael Joseph; Andre Deutsch Ltd for 'I'm the youngest in our house' from *Wouldn't You Like to Know* by Michael Rosen; *Chapter 18* The author for 'The Huntsman' by Edward Lowbury; *Chapter 19*: SCDC Publications for 'Tim's blackbird diary' from *Writing and Learning across the Curriculum* by Nancy Martin et al, Ward Lock Educational 1976; *Chapter 21*: IPC Magazines Ltd for 'Creepy Crawler' from *School Fun*, 21 January 1984; *Chapters 25, 27 and 29*: The Royal National Institute for the Deaf for poster, 'He never hears a word his mother says. And he never will.'; *Chapter 26*: The author for 'My father's father' by Michael Rosen; Andre Deutsch Ltd for 'Newcomers' from *Quick, Let's Get Out of Here* by Michael Rosen; *Chapter 30*: Methuen Children's Books for extracts and illustrations from *Flat Stanley* by Jeff Brown, illustrated by Tomi Ungerer; Ward Lock Educational Ltd for extracts from *Flat Stanley* adapted by Sheila Lane and Marion Kemp. The Publishers have made every effort to clear copyrights and trust that their apologies will be accepted for any errors or omissions. They will be pleased to hear from any copyright holder who has not received due acknowledgement, though where no reply was received to their letters requesting permission, the Publishers have assumed that there was no objection to their using the material.